YOU'RE GRAND

The Irishwoman's Secret Guide to Life

TARA FLYNN

HACHETTE
BOOKS
IRELAND

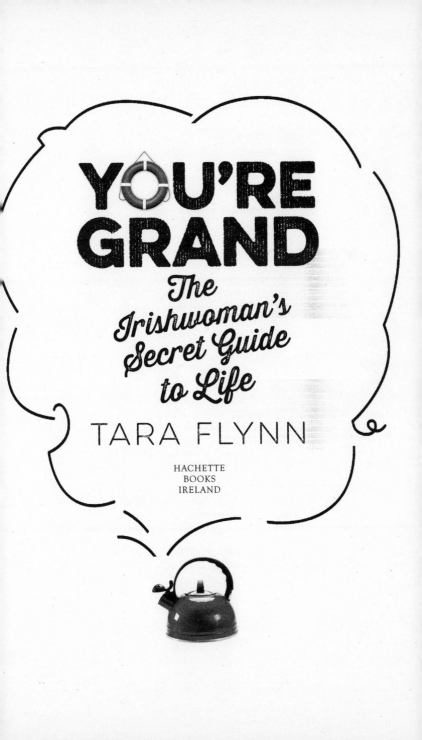

First published in Ireland in 2014 by
HACHETTE BOOKS IRELAND

10 9 8 7 6 5 4 3 2

Copyright © Tara Flynn 2014

A CIP catalogue record for this book is available from the British Library.

ISBN 978 1 444797732

Typeset in Granjon by www.cabinlondon.co.uk
Photographs © Shutterstock/Ist Gallery (life belt) © Michel Dzierzynski/
Shutterstock (kettle) ©/Danny Smythe/Shutterstock (teapot)

Printed and bound in Great Britain by CPI Group (UK) Ltd,
Croydon, CRO 4YY

Hachette Books Ireland policy is to use papers that are natural, renewable
and recyclable products and made from wood grown in sustainable
forests. The logging and manufacturing processes are expected to conform
to the environmental regulations of the country of origin.

Hachette Books Ireland
8 Castlecourt Centre
Castleknock
Dublin 15, Ireland
A division of Hachette UK Ltd
338 Euston Road, London NW1 3BH
www.hachette.ie

★

For all the Irishwomen out there.
Be you born in Ireland, of Irish descent,
newly arrived, would-be Irish,
would-be women.
This book is a guide to how to reach your
full Irishwomanly potential.

★

Contents

·····★·····

3
GRAND BASICS (A STARTER PACK)

59

4

KNOWING YOUR PLACE

105

5
GRAND HOBBIES AND PASTIMES
157

6
LOOKING GRAND, FEELING GRAND:
FASHION, HEALTH AND BEAUTY
183

7
GRAND SEX
219

8
YOU'RE GRAND:
THE SECRETS REVEALED

265

•••••★•••••

GRAND THANKS

FÁILTE:
A Grand Welcome

You're Grand: The State of Mind

Irish women are awesome, and it's well known that we're terribly wise. And you've picked up this book because you want to know our secret. Welcome. You've come to the right place. Quite a few of us have been Irish women for ages and things have worked out pretty much OK.

Until now, there haven't been a lot of Irish self-help books. In Ireland, there's a perception that if you're helping yourself, you must have too much free time on your hands. You must not be sound. Here, a 'life path' is the route that gets you safely over the mountain; a 'life coach' is one that doesn't have to stop for petrol in Athlone. It's simply not possible for us to not Sweat the Small Stuff, with glands the size of ours.

But what every Irishwoman instinctively knows is that, no matter how bad things get, sooner or later everything will be Grand. Even when it won't. In fact, especially then. Simply asserting that "You're Grand" puts you in a state of mind that

TARA FLYNN

instantly makes you feel better, even in the face of disaster, grief, or 800 years of oppression at the hand of a near neighbour. Irish women have lived through all of these. And we're Grand. We really are very wise.

It's high time we shared this state of mind, this wisdom – the secret to being Grand – with the rest of the world. If you aren't feeling Grand just yet, even if you're not yet sure quite what it means, this book will change your life.

Irish women have always been helpers. There has always been someone to save from some kind of cliff-related death, bankruptcy or soup-taking. But when it comes to helping *ourselves*, we get a bit flummoxed. We're just not used to it. Something about all that irrepressible positivity makes us uncomfortable, so if we are going to read self-help books, we only read them on holidays. Like baguettes optimistically purchased in Paris, self-help books don't travel back to Ireland well.

But wise *and* generous, Irish women certainly don't mind passing on what we've learned about being Grand. We know that if we can be Grand after all the shite we've had to put up with, anyone can.

Other guides to life like *The Secret* will tell you that you can have whatever you want. Well, Irish women know that you can't. Forget wishing and hoping and cutting things out of a magazine to manifest them: all that manifests is a holey magazine. That's just wasteful. Other life-guides can also seem

to suggest that if something goes wrong or a desire fails to manifest, you're doing it wrong – you're not being positive hard enough (or maybe you cut stuff out of the wrong magazine). Not this life-guide. Irish women would never be so foolhardy as to trust in a good outcome in the first place. We know that it actually doesn't matter whether things turn out good or bad (most likely bad): either way we'll be Grand.

To sum up, in terms of yet another famous life-guide, if *French Women Don't Get Fat*, Irish Women Don't Get Cold: we just put on a jumper and get on with it, perfectly Grand.

You're Grand is the only life-guide you'll ever need and the theories are much less makey-uppy than most of the rest of them. It's an only-partly-makey-uppy journey through how Irish women have managed to not only survive but thrive during what really is an awful lot of nonsense by anyone's standards.

Let's face it, life can be miserable: well, misery always goes better with an Irishwoman around.

So if you're an Irishwoman, or just want to be like one, or if you feel you need a reminder that everything will, in fact, be Grand, this is the book for you. And here's the first secret: you're already there. Everything is alright. You're Grand.

Grand: The Meaning

• • • • •

Irish women say they're "Grand" about a million times a day. But let's be clear, it doesn't mean "fancy": It simply means the bare bones of "fine". In Ireland, the word "Grand" isn't confined to ballrooms, candelabras or horsey types: it's not elaborate, not highfalutin, just fine.

Now, I want you to say this aloud: <u>Being fine is a fantastic aspiration</u>. As an Irishwoman, you certainly wouldn't ask for much more. That'd be taking the piss.

We'll mainly be talking about 'Grand' in this sense, the sense of being calm, centred and at your most Irishly fine. Not great, but kind of OK. But just in case you're still not clear on its meaning, here's 'Grand' in context.

• • • • • ★ • • • • •

SCENARIO:
Paying at the Newsagent's:

"Hello, Mary. How are you today?"

"I'm grand."

"Oh dear. Just grand?"

"Yeah. I'm just after giving myself a paper cut on these *Ireland's Own*s. But I'll live."

"They're a hoor for the edges, alright."

As you can see, Mary could be having a better day, but she hasn't cut the hand off herself. There's a pessimistic optimism at play. She is GRAND. So that's what she says.

When used in conjunction with "You're" – as in "You're Grand" – grand can be very soothing. Reassuring. It means "Don't worry about it." Or "It's not your fault."

As in:

> "I'm sorry you got a paper cut when I handed you those Ireland's Owns I should have turned them around."
> "Ah, you're grand. Sure, they're a hoor for the edges."

If you still haven't got the hang of it, don't worry. It'll soak in eventually, after years of putting up with stuff. Even people living in Ireland 20 years or more still think it means "splendid" or "great", until contradicted by miserable faces and wet shoes.

Grand is at its most powerful when used in the face of complete devastation. Awfulness that cannot be reversed. You must still say you're Grand. Your teeth may be gritted, but you must still say it. Written off your car? You're Grand. Lost your winning Euromillions ticket? You're Grand. Confined to your holiday bed with explosive diarrhoea? Still Grand.

It doesn't change a thing, but saying you're Grand somehow deepens your acceptance of a situation and brings you peace and contentment. Well, maybe not the contentment. But peace will do, won't it? We could all use a little extra peace. Sometimes it's just easier to go with the flow of the bad situation, and, as a result, the outcome will be the slow-dawning realisation that, actually, You're Grand.

A Few Variations on the Grand Theme:

★ **GRAND OUT**: Nothing to do with whether she's indoors or out, an Irishwoman who is really pretty happy with how things are right now is said to be "Grand out". E.g. curled up on the couch by the fire on a wet day, or not being told to be quiet.

★ **GRAND ALTOGETHER**: Being Grand altogether might be being a bit too Grand. Approach such complacency with caution. An Irishwoman knows that things are probably about to go wrong again very soon and so – although things will ultimately be Grand – if she's feeling "Grand altogether" she should be prepared for a knock.

★ **GRAHND**: Say this in an English accent, with a bit of a sneer. This is Grand as the rest

of the world knows it: fancy, posh, above one's station. Not a good thing.

★ **THAT'S GRAND**: This means "leave off the work there; it'll do". It means never, ever going the extra mile – you won't get any thanks for it. You'll only wear yourself out trying to excel, so one of the best things about being Grand is you can stop working on something as soon as you can get away with it; covering over cracks, not bothering to train for a job or event, insisting the fish is fresh and local even when the microwave can be heard pinging in the distance: all Grand. This immediately eliminates a lot of the stress experienced in other countries.

A word of caution: **BEWARE** if the vowel in "Grand" is extended. "*I'm graaaaand*." Then the "A" has become sarcastic. The speaker is *not* Grand, far from it, and you're probably somehow to blame – particularly if "*I'm graaaaand*" is followed by an uncomfortable silence. Run. Further: one of the most dangerous sounds that could possibly come from an Irishwoman is: "*You're graaaaand*." It means it *is* your fault, you know what you did

and you should probably never have come into this newsagent's in the first place.

Grand Men

Before we get too far into our journey, a quick word on our male counterparts. There will be accusations that any book focussed on women must be anti-men, and that men are awful and that we're all locked in cupboards and that they did it. That absolutely isn't the case. In fact, there's nothing to suggest we can't all be the best Irish women we can be, men included.

Irish men are also awesome. There have been misguided moments in their history – when they wouldn't let us into pubs, for instance – but that's over now. To be honest, if I could have a pub to myself, I'd probably take it too. Before that, we were all equally squished under British rule. Men shared our pain. In fact, some of the secrets in this book are secrets our fellas know too. Being Grand isn't a solely female preserve. It's just that Irish women have needed to put the secrets of being Grand into practice more often.

Even further back, in Ancient Times, Irish men held us up as goddesses and queens without our even having to ask. How cool is that? We really do have a lot to thank them for.

24

So when we say "they" in this book with regard to squishing or shushing or whatever, we're not talking about men in general: we're talking about gender-irrelevant bad apples who squished and shushed us because it suited them. Many of them happened to be men, but not you. We're not talking about you. You're Grand.

Nowadays, when Irish women go on one of our many protest marches, there are loads of men walking with us and they don't seem to mind sharing the pubs at all. They even buy us the odd pint and let us buy one back. And they're very handsome now they've started combing the hair since the recent demise of the cloth cap.

We love Irish men. Call us sexist for that if you like.

What Makes An Irishwoman

• • • • •

Like in Dana's uncharacteristically inclusive Eurovision song, there are all kinds of Irish women these days. It's a beautiful thing. We come in all colours, shapes, sizes, sexual orientations and – at long last – we're beginning to hear transgender women's voices. Hurrah! There's plenty of room for all of us, since the Famine and constant emigration left a lot of space in the country. We might as well fill it up.

Wherever you're originally from and no matter what your external manifestation, the broader guidelines for being Grand like an Irishwoman remain the same for all of us.

According to the rhyme, little girls are made from sugar and spice and all things nice. That just doesn't work here: sugar and spice would dissolve too quickly in the rain, and we're not nice. Awesome, yes. Nice, no.

Irish women – be they gay, straight, born here, born abroad, learning Irish, currently identifying as female – are made of the same stuff: hope, craic, waterproof material, turf, bacon products, limestone, iron and wool. No sugar, no spice and not a shamrock in sight. But every single one of us is absolutely Grand with that.

Sise

The Irish word (*Gaelic, foreign friends, is known as Irish here*) for "herself" is *sise*. When pronounced correctly, it's essentially someone saying "sh" twice in quick succession.

Try it: *Sh-sh*.

That's it.

So even our own language indicated that we were to be seen and not heard, and then if we were to be seen it should only be while collecting eggs or partly obscured by a harp.

"*Shh*" is a sound that Irish women have heard a lot, until pretty recently:

Shh! Don't get above your station or lose the run of yourself.

Shh! You're not English.

Shh! Don't tell anyone you're pregnant: they'll know you had sex.

Shh! Drink more quietly or they'll know there's a woman in this pub.

Shh! Raising your voice is unladylike.

Shh! I'm not supposed to give you this family planning information so you ain't seen me, right?

Shh! No one needs to overhear your confession. You're not saying anything juicy.

Shh! This is a funeral. Don't be having <u>too</u> much craic.

Shh! Quiet there now, like a good girleen, and get me another drop o' the black shtuff. None for you, though.

Amazingly for a group so gifted with the gab, Irish women have traditionally seemed to comply with this shushing, which really isn't Grand. "Seemed to" being the operative words. As soon as we were out of earshot we'd be chatting up a storm and plotting our revenge.

> ★ In case you didn't know, the Irish word for "woman" is *"bean"* (pronounced "ban") with the plural being "mná" (pronounced like a cat being put through a wood chipper). For such fascinating creatures, we really have been given ugly words to describe us.

How To Connect with Your Inner Grandness
(A MEDITATION)

•••••

In order to connect with what you're about to learn in as effective a way as possible, you'll need to place yourself in the Grand state of mind. This will make you more receptive to the Grand as you proceed through the book.

Sit quietly in a darkened room with your shoes off and some gentle music or chanting in the background. This will immediately give you a sense of what it's like to be a traditional Irishwoman. Breathe in and breathe out. Even when things are awful you'll usually be able to do this part, so no harm having a bit of a practice now. Think of any problems you have. Let them come into your mind. See them. Feel them. Now, far from turning them into clouds and letting them dissipate, or visualising happy-coloured balloons that float away, let those worries get right up in your face – maybe they have terrifying, pointy teeth – before tying you into a giant knot of frustration and despair. Breathe in, breathe out. Sit there in your knot for a while. It will feel awful. But then, look down. Is there a puddle of mud under you? No, there isn't. There's no mud in your mind. So you're Grand. This tiny bit of relief will cause you to

stop struggling against the knot. You realise it's not so tight after all, and that it's actually giving you a bit of a yoga stretch. So you're Grand. In the knotty stillness, from beyond the music or chanting and deep inside yourself, you begin to hear a rhythmic sound. It's the sound of your heart. "Boom boom. Boom boom," it says. But now, for perhaps the first time in your life, you realise what your heart is saying to you: "Boom boom. Boom boom. You're Grand. You're Grand." Even when you're under stress and your heart starts to beat faster, it's just telling you You're Grand at a faster rate and more times per minute at a time you might need to hear it a bit more often.

So, anytime you feel alone, sad or confused, be still, breathe in and breathe out and just listen: from deep in your own heart you'll receive the only two words of wisdom you need. You're Grand.

2

GRAND
HISTORY:
*Things Haven't
Always Been Grand*

★

A Grand Brief History

The problem with Irish history is that there's just so fecking much of it. Too many dates and names and places – ugh. Who – apart from American relatives – has the time? So here's a potted history of what's happened to Irish women, events Grand and not so Grand, up to this point. If you like that kind of thing.

PRE-HISTORY/ANCIENT TIMES: In the beginning, we were tiny, tiny people who lived in ring forts. We know we were tiny because when they reconstruct ring forts, the doors are very, very low. Seriously, Kylie Minogue would have to stoop to go into one, so it's just as well she wasn't around at the time.

If she were, though, there'd have been loads to take her mind off her great height. These were

better-than-Grand times for women in Ireland. Although we had little more than cloaks and brooches, women were in charge! We were allowed to boss everyone about, even when it came to important stuff. We made good use of our power and had a great time doing it. That said, Queen Meadbh may have been the straw that broke the camel's – or the bull's – back by creating a mythological war over livestock. Her bad track record with cattle probably had a lot to do with our fall from grace, and subsequent overreliance on agriculture.

VIKINGS & NORMANS: Then came the Vikings (hot) and the Normans (classy, terrible name). Our downfall continued due to these conquerors being mostly blokes, and blokes with axes at that. There was also a rise in the numbers of holy fellas up and down the land, telling us to shush. A great shushening fell upon us. Our cards were marked and they were red: we were off the pitch. Benched wenches. This went on for literally Ages.

THE ENGLISH: were kind of mean to every-body in the past, regardless of gender, so instead of "800 years of oppression", you could say we had 800 years of equality with our lads. Progressive.

There was a huge Famine – you've probably

heard of it – known as the Great Famine. But it wasn't great; it wasn't even Grand. Our potatoes got blighted and we either starved or went to America. These really weren't the most craic of times.

During these lean years for Irish women there was the odd breakout success: actresses, patriots and doers of good works, but as there are so few monuments to them, you'd be forgiven for not knowing they existed. Maybe there was a plaque shortage as well as a potato blight. Probably just as well: if we had as many commemorative statues and portraits of brilliant women as we do of men, we wouldn't be able to move. The traffic's bad enough as it is and look at the kerfuffle that ensued when they moved Molly Malone.

20TH CENTURY: The rise of suffrage internationally coincided with the uprising of the Irish against the British Crown. Women regained some of their feistiness around that time and were active (if largely unsung) in the 1916 Rising and the newly formed trade unions.

But, just in case we'd let the power go to our heads and lost the run of ourselves, the Church stepped in and made sure we remembered what terrible sinners we were. Every woman was prone

to losing the run of herself, but some in particular needed extra special attention. Young single mothers were made to live in mother-and-baby homes or in Magdalene laundries, had their babies taken from them, and were forced to starch wimples to keep them busy and out of the way of trouble and penises. It was a great way of straightening out wayward women altogether – not to mention getting convent whites that dazzling *blue white*! Yes, it does look a bit like slavery, now you mention it. Reparation has yet to be paid and I don't think Church whites have looked as white since, to be honest.

In the '90s and 2000s came the golden era of the Two Marys, Robinson and McAleese. Irish Presidents don't have power to change that much, but their symbolic rule gave us hope.

We finally got divorce, and homosexuality was decriminalised. In the '90s. The *1990s*. We finally got access to contraception, but we still don't have full bodily autonomy. Some of us aren't too happy about the legislation in that regard (including, you know, the UN), but still, two out of three ain't bad. It's grand for now. There's more marching to be done, but as you'll see, sure we enjoy a good walk.

And that concludes our whirlwind tour of the history of the

Irishwoman. What does the future hold? Hard to say. But hopefully something along the lines of more unblighted potatoes, more say over what happens to our own bodies and less of someone else's laundry.

Ah Sure, Feck It

•••••

The first and most important secret of how to be the best Irishwoman you can be is a lesson in language. WAIT, DON'T GO! I'm not going to attempt to teach you Irish; it's very complex and also I'm terrible at it. Blame Peig. (More on that later in *We Need to Talk About Peig*.)

"Grand" isn't the only word Irish women have that's exclusive to us. This next word is a doozy. It's simple and easy to say, but its effect is profound. If you don't live in Ireland, you may have heard it from Father Jack in *Father Ted*, so it should be familiar enough. I'm going to need you to say it aloud with me, right now, and if you're on board – if you're really committed to being Grand – you'll join in. Come on, repeat after me, say it. SAY IT!

"FECK"

•••••

You probably feel like you've said a bad word, don't you? If you were reading this on public transport, you might even have skipped the saying it aloud bit, you cheat, you. Because it feels

impolite. It feels powerful and shocking. But get this: it isn't bad at all! You can say "Feck" in front of anyone, even a priest! Father Jack himself said it multiple times in a sitting.

"Feck" is a great release of frustration, when there simply isn't a nearby cliff to shout off the top of. "Feck", like "Grand" in many ways, is one of the keys to Irish women's power. Which is a lot of influence for a word someone made up so they could swear when priests were around.

Feck isn't just "fuck" with an "e", though. We've turned it into a philosophy of life. A further route to being Grand. Irish women all know when to say "Ah sure, feck it": when to walk away from a fight, or when to stick around for the last bit of cake, even though you're not supposed to. It's knowing when something's not worth it, or is just worth it enough. It's being strong, and giving in, all at the same time. It's magic.

•••••★•••••

WHEN TO SAY "AH SURE, FECK IT"

Your friend has made fresh scones. You're one of those people who pretend to be allergic to gluten. Ah sure, feck it – you have a feckin' scone.

Ireland are playing on a weekday. It doesn't matter what sport. You're working. Ah sure, feck it – you ring in sick.

You've been told again and again to be quiet like a good girl. Ah sure, feck it – not a chance.

It's raining, and you've glammed up for the evening. Ah sure, feck it – hair dries fierce quick when you're having a good time.

It's cold. Ah sure, feck it – with the trusty jumper all good Irish women have on, you won't even notice.

You've been dumped by an awful eejit. Ah sure, feck it – plenty more eejit-fish in the sea.

You're not allowed to become a priest. Ah sure, feck it – the job description's not what it used to be, anyway.

Thing is, you can always walk away. If you didn't know that before, you know it now. If you'd forgotten it, it's time to remember it. Too much post to be opened? Too many carrots to purée? Too much shite on the telly? Feck that. It'll still be there in a while if you want. If something doesn't make sense or is just no craic, it's no longer a problem. You'll feel Grand if you just say … FECK IT.

Breaking Bold: A Grand Contradiction in Terms

• • • • •

You'll have started to notice that part of our charm lies in our contradictory nature. (No it doesn't. Yes it does.) Being strong and giving in at the same time sort of sums us up. We're a people who've been taught not to speak out of turn, not to rock the boat, and to do our best to please. BUT ... Well, let's have a look at that big BUT.

Irish women have always been told to do things "like a good girl". Even in situations where the action could be completed by any kind of girl at all, good or not, e.g. "Pass me the salt, like a good girl." It seems it was felt that Irish girls had to be constantly reminded not to be evil, even when doing something as basic as handling condiments. Boys don't get asked to do things *like good boys*. More than a little unfair, if you ask me.

But it was probably just as well, because traditional, old Ireland was *right*. We *aren't* to be trusted. We have something going on deep within us that means we can never, ever be good girls, even if we want to. Even if we try. Be good? Ah sure, feck that. Being Grand means you just can't be good all the time.

It's not that we're bad either – far from it. But I'll tell you what we are: we're *bold*.

Boldness is another key to the You're Grand state of mind. Being *bold* in Ireland doesn't mean fearless, or courageous, or brazen (although of course there's a bit of those in there too). Here, *bold* has an added dash of naughtiness. Divilment. Sass. Bold means forgoing being good in favour of a bit of craic.

Nobody wants to be no craic. Or nice, for that matter. To an Irishwoman, being told "you're nice" is an insult: nice is too safe. Nice is a mischief-free zone. Nice won't do at all.

Being bold doesn't mean being nasty. It's the glint in your eye, or the spring in your step when you borrow your sister's new shoes without asking. Here's a helpful chart:

BOLD	BAD
Borrowing without asking	Stealing
A little white lie	Hurting someone's feelings
Descriptive arm-flailing accidents	Damaging stuff
Winding up doorstep canvassers	Becoming a politician for the "wrong party"
Chocolate stains	Littering

BOLD	BAD
Eating a bit of icing off a birthday cake	Forgetting a birthday
Flirting	Flirting with someone else's partner
Carbs	Diets
Pretending you're away, but staying home and peeping out the windows, people-watching	Pretending you're home, but going away
Cheering for another county's team because you fancy someone from Mayo	Forgetting an important match
Deleting something from the DVR because it's full of old matches, and *Buffy the Vampire Slayer* is "just so well written."	Not liking *Buffy the Vampire Slayer*. What's wrong with you?

Boldness is the spice of life. It's how adventures happen. When a parent says to a child, "Don't be bold," they're secretly hoping they'll get a call from the school telling them you weren't paying attention during *Peig* (more on Peig below) because you were fashioning an escape-currach under the desk.

Boldness isn't just about the craic, though. It's more important than that. It's a kind of force field. It's why, despite all the attempts

to squish and shush Irish women throughout history, we bounce back. We do our best to be obedient, to serve and to please, but something deep in our nature is constantly tugging at us, telling us to *feck that*.

Without boldness, we might have been shh-ed out of all existence by now. Or worse: be no craic. So take it from us. Break Bold.

Real Housewives of the Blaskets: We Need to Talk About Peig

•••••

"I'm an old woman now, with one foot in the grave and another on its edge." If you don't recognise that quote, if it hasn't struck terror into your heart, then we have some catching up to do. Those of you who have been going "Who's Peig?". You, my young, untainted friends, are the lucky ones.

For those of us who know of her, the mere mention of Peig's name brings on uncontrollable twitching. A chill down our spines. A fear that we've somehow forgotten a 30-year-old Irish essay assignment and it's due in the morning.

To those having adverse reactions, apologies. But we need to talk about her. Sorry. We have to.

At one time, every teenager in Ireland was taught *Peig* (the autobiography of Peig Sayers of the Great Blasket Island, who

lived from 1873 to 1958). We say "taught"; it was more that we were lashed screaming to a tree, eyes propped open with twigs and forced to read aloud this "treasured" story of misery, emigration and loss. In IRISH.

I'm going to go out on a limb and say that one of the main reasons so few people speak our beautiful native language is *Peig*. It's her and her autobiography's fault. Associating Irish directly with graves and moaning when all we wanted was to snog the face off someone at the school disco, meant that the woman's name induced sighing, eye-rolling and excessively enthusiastic speaking of English.

Peig was a great collector of folklore and island traditions, and she was accepted as a *seanchaí* (storyteller) at a time when few women were. This is all Grand. She was visited by great tragedy – including the time one of her sons blew off a Blasket cliff. In a sad indication of the level of misery fatigue you've reached by that point in the story, this episode gets a laugh. Sounds awful, I know, but it's true. Poor Peig. But more to the point, poor teenage us.

Peig was what we were taught real Irish women should be like: "Never on the island again will there be a woman as Irish as me." Obedient, delighted to be miserable, shawl-wearing and giving no back chat – except for the odd hilarious story of somebody dying, told from the middle of the fireplace.

She has a lot to answer for, so we're going to have to pay her a visit.

44

Below is a quick tour of Peig's world. I would call these "cliff notes" but for obvious reasons that would be inappropriate.

•••••★•••••

PEIG FAQ

Wasn't she just some nice old lady who told stories?
NO. That's just what they'd like you to think.
This "nice old lady" ruined more than just Irish for everyone. "I'm an old woman now ..." is the very first line of *Peig* and things only get cheerier from there. NOT. Peig survived hard hardship after harder hardship only to end up living in hardship on Hardship Island, because hardship. In the glamour stakes the above description is *Real Housewives of the Blaskets* compared to the real thing.

But if she was such a survivor, isn't she sound?
NO. Peig showed little – if any – boldness. She put up with her lot like a good girl, accepting every scrap of hardship dealt to her, then making sure to moan about it for ages, using plenty of alliteration. She is often referred to as "salt of the earth", as someone who "tells it like it is", which actually means telling it like it isn't, but loud.

Isn't her sacrifice for others inspiring?
It's true, Peig agrees to be put into domestic service

("slavery" – calm down, Peig) because she's a burden on her family. The chapter is called "I Am a Cause of Strife." Yes, Peig. That might be a clue.

Peig seems to have been lazy and a bit of a mean girl. Stuff like "… but that didn't bother me as long as it was convenient for myself." Classic Peig. Twice she finds dead bodies that ultimately turn out not to be dead at all, but Peig would rather run into a house screaming "He's dead, God help us!" and start planning the wake than check for a pulse. Or, you know, *help*.

But she has a strong sense of community, surely?
Maybe, but mainly she's worried about herself. Worst of all, she's no fan of the sisterhood. "Women are the devil himself for causing disturbance." Oh, she doesn't like us at all. Peig moans about almost all the other women who cross her path unless they're called Cáit – which luckily, due to a shortage of Irish parents that give a shite about names* (* See Grand Names), most of them are.

I heard she was great fun in real life. Isn't there any comic relief?
At one point, Peig nearly drowns a cow in a ditch. She thinks it's hilarious. But don't you worry! Grimness is never far behind.

OTHER HIGHLIGHTS

★ Her match is made with someone she's never seen, someone dies tragically so – wouldn't you know it – their wedding becomes a wake.

★ Taking in a beautiful view with her mother, they chat about a family burned alive in their cottage. Then they skip in for their tea.

★ Her BFF, the best one of all the Cáits, is supposed to send her money to bring her to America. Tragically for all of us, she doesn't.

★ Babies are born, loads of them, but no one ever, ever has sex. *Peig* was one of the first official places where modern Irish girls learned that Sex was a dirty word. In the hundreds and hundreds of words of Peig's interminable misery-fest, it doesn't appear at all. So dirty, it cannot be named. Thanks, Peig.

Obviously, it was hoped we'd overlook the odd flyaway child and be subliminally drawn back to the ways of the late 19th and early 20th centuries, handing in our bras and votes in exchange for forbearance and a bit of Shop Bread at Christmas. (Peig is mad for it, so I can only assume that "Shop Bread" is some kind of narcotic being dealt out of Dingle.) Sadly for

Peig, we'd grown too fond of the aul' progress for that.

If our boldness hadn't shielded us and kept us moving forward, here's how a woman's life in Ireland might read today, Peig stylee:

•••••★•••••

A Day in the Life of the Modern Peig

The times are hard now, not like they were in times gone by, like 2004, but better than they were in older times like the 1980s. In those times there was no teeth-whitening or talk of teeth-whitening. The work now is hard and many the poor crater suffers RSI and blurred vision and a splayed arse from long days making job applications online. I had taken a queer kind of a notion to be going into town of a Saturday, devil take me, and sure I wasn't long in before I was being jostled and pushed by young people out and about and they with the sup of drink taken. I went to see would I find anyone I would know in the old places, but sure they were all long gone to Australia and we hear no talk of them now, except on Skype the odd time. I got it into my head to go home on the bus, but sure wasn't the blasted thing diverted due to some protest. Someone said it was some women, bad cess to them, protesting that they wanted more than what they have now when

haven't we plenty, and we not locked in a dungeon.
They say a protesting woman is like a cow in a ditch,
half drowned and there no rain. A bus did come, but
a young fella pushed me out of the way and it full.
Wasn't it the right shove I gave him before the doors
closed, and he smashing his face on the driver's booth,
losing his two front teeth. "Instagram that,"
says I to myself, and I laughing and I going down the
road, the two feet under me. There was no Instagram
in my day, or talk of Instagram. Whatever it was about
me, I walked home the 5 miles and when I got there
didn't I wash my feet, for the last time a woman could
afford shoes was 2008. Before getting into bed, alone,
and with no television for to stimulate me further than
the day's adventures, I tore a handful off the Shop
Bread I'd been carrying around in my pocket and
shoved it into me gob. I'd a grand glow on me now,
because the peelers never caught me with the Shop
Bread and I in town the whole day. Bad cess to them.
Sure 'tis all I have. High as a kite on the white flour,
I blew out my candle, and went to sleep hoping I
wouldn't die anytime in the next 5 minutes to 50 years.
But, knowing my luck, I would.

Happily, most Irish women were too bold to even bother finishing
Peig and so weren't taken in by it.

A good rule of thumb for modern Irish women is to ask "What Would Peig Do?" and then do the opposite. Get yourself a wristband, say it aloud daily. WWPD? Then don't do it. If nothing else, your cattle will be safer.

Forgive and Forget: The Elephants of Europe

•••••

It's not so long ago that boarding houses in the UK and US posted signs saying "No Blacks. No dogs. No Irish". We were below dogs on the list but as you can see, we've totally let it go. NOT. We're Irish – we don't let anything go. Old *Punch* cartoons used to depict us as some sort of pig people. Not only offensive but inaccurate: Irish people are not pigs. We're elephants. Because elephants never forget.

Look at how often we've mentioned the Famine and the Catholic Church in this life-guide already, when – apart from getting to the chip van too late after a gig, or the odd clatter on the back of the legs from a nun – many of us aren't affected directly anymore.

Irish people have two memories: personal and collective. And we take our collective history personally. And that is why we have such a complex relationship with England. It's why we'll still mutter "800 years of oppression" under our breath if

an English pal is even a few minutes late for a coffee date.

Most English people today would be terrible oppressors: they're too busy watching *Strictly Come Dancing* or trying to save the NHS. They haven't done anything bad to us and half of them aren't even aware of what their ancestors got up to.

The Queen came over 3 years ago and spoke Irish, bowed and made almost everything OK between us. But still, we elephants can't let go. But it's time. More than time. If we don't let go, how can we be Grand? I think the following will help.

WHY WE SHOULD THANK THE ENGLISH:

• • • • •

★ They outlawed Catholicism long before any of the scandals that have recently driven many Catholics from the Church. They were only looking out for us, in advance.

★ Masses were driven underground, held in fields with large boulders for altars, known as Mass Rocks. These were precursors to and great training for festivals like Electric Picnic – and I'd like to propose "Mass Rocks" as a new slogan for the Church.

★ They sold our good crops for profit and left us with just potatoes. Which are the bit of the meal we really like best anyway. So that was nice of them.

★ While we starved, they made cartoons depicting us as pigs or apes in stovepipe hats. Probably because they knew how much we like craic and self-deprecation. Nothing staves off a hunger pang like a good old laugh!

★ They forced us to learn and speak their language. We weren't very happy about it at the time, but you have to admit that the old English is very handy all the same. You won't find too many fluent Gaeilgeoirí in Times Square.

★ For ages, we only had one TV channel. Reading in comics and magazines about glamorous shows like *Coronation Street* and *Doctor Who* gave us hope beyond *The Late Late Show*.

★ They have snakes. We have no snakes. They could easily have brought them over on the ferry but they didn't.

★ They do our accent at us. Badly. It's hilarious and gives us a great lift.

★ They must have talked shite about us to the Romans, because the Romans never came here, even though they were right next door. They probably thought we'd get on great with the Italians and the two of us would gang up on them, so they talked

them out of invading. But whatever the motivation, we're grateful, because the last thing we needed at the time was yet another oppressor.

★ They made us soup* (see box below) when we were starving. Sure, you had to stop being a Catholic and you lost your Irish name if you took it, but soup worth being disowned for must have been absolutely delicious.

Lots to be grateful to the English for, as you can see. It's high time for us elephants to ditch the trunks that are our emotional baggage. Bitterness is a terrible accessory.

But still. 800 years.

• • • • • ★ • • • • •

Taking The Soup

During Famine times, Protestant and Quaker soup kitchens were set up to feed starving Catholics. It's not known what flavours were on offer, but potato is unlikely to have been one of them.

If you gave in and took the soup, you were definitely a Protestant (in fact, you had to become one), so you'd be shunned by your own people for the crime of cosying up to the landowners who'd taken your food from you in the first place. Shunned

is not a good look. If you became a "Souper", you had your Irishness symbolically lifted from you, as the community removed the "O" or "Mac" from your name.

The rumour that these missing letters were then used to make a very limited alphabet soup has not been corroborated.

★

The Seven Ages of a Grand Irishwoman

With that bit of background in mind, you're almost ready to embark on life as an Irishwoman, and a Grand life altogether it'll be. Here's a taster of what's in store during the various phases of that life:

1. BIRTH: You're here! *Fáilte!* You're very welcome. Now, before we go any further – we're sorry. You've landed in Ireland. You're going to be cold and wet and there will almost definitely be some oppression. But don't worry, you'll be having plenty of craic to make up for it. Now, let's get you baptised *immediately.* Just lie back and enjoy the refreshing near-drowning and attendant party, with special guest appearances from every member of your family there to "wet the baby's head". Get a

good look at them while you can. You will never see most of these people again.

2. INFANCY: You've made it this far, which means it must either be the 20th century or later, or you have the genes of an ox. By now, you should be picking up loads of words and phrases due to the incessant chat all around you. Try to start walking as soon as possible: you'll want to start hearing the phrase "she's a great walker" for the first time. But definitely not the last.

3. CHILDHOOD: By now you're almost definitely a Catholic (or having to pretend to be one to get into your nearest school) but if you're not, don't worry. Weirdos and normal children play perfectly well together at this stage. Be sure and make your First Holy Communion by the time you're 7 so you get into the training of spending hundreds or even thousands of euro on an event; this will stand you in good stead come your inevitable wedding day. It's never too early to start thinking about being an Irish Mother, or "Mammy".

4. ADOLESCENCE: You have now run out of time to correct your many flaws; whatever's wrong with you at this stage will go with you to the grave. So, feck it. By now you should have met your future husband and if you haven't then you really aren't taking this whole thing seriously enough. Alternatively, you can move to Brussels to be an interpreter: they put up with all kinds of weirdos there and the *moules frites*

are fantastic. Honestly – mussels with chips: hard to believe it isn't our own national dish.

5. IRISH MOTHER OR MAMMY: Hurrah! You've finally achieved your life-long dream – or come to your senses after a couple of harsh years in Belgium. Now you're a Real Irishwoman, and not a minute too soon. But if at this stage it turns out you haven't become a mum, don't worry. You can always be a teacher (almost a mammy), an air hostess (the mammy of the skies), or you can go back to Belgium. It isn't very far, at the end of the day, and the waffles are fantastic if you're getting sick of the *moules*.

6. RETIREMENT: You can never retire. This shit is for life.

7. PEIG: Finally. You can be who you were always meant to be. This is your destiny. You can let all your teeth fall out, get off your bin on Shop Bread, make everyone else's life a misery and still get tons of respect. You don't even have to go and live on a remote island to be more like Peig: YOU ALREADY LIVE ON A REMOTE ISLAND: Ireland. So sit back and let the nose hair kick in. Tell the odd story, steal the odd thing and poke people with your stick. Everyone will say you're "a character" and smile. This truly is the best phase for Irish women. Just make sure you talk about death every day. But then, you do that anyway.

A Dirty Word

·····

Here comes that tug again! On the one hand, what we're meant to aspire to (according to the old lads), and on the other, what we're really like. You'll probably have noticed a glaring omission from the Seven Ages of a Grand Irishwoman there. SEX. It's been almost as absent as it was in *Peig*. Don't worry. It's coming. Sex has featured very prominently in our history: having it, not being allowed to have it, being forced to transform from lusty pagans to uptight biddies and not being very happy about it. The having it or not having it is part of what defines us. I'd go so far as to say that it underpins almost everything that's happened to us historically, and is part of the spark of boldness that's kept us sane. There's nothing quite as bold as sex. So we can't just go rushing straight to secrets about sex, ripping off our shawls as we go: we have to work up to it. You'll have to spend a bit of time with Irish women first, getting to know us, finding out what we like, before you get a glimpse under the jumper. We will build to it, but slowly. It's always better that way.

We wish you a long and happy life as an Irishwoman. You may be a bit nervous about what lies ahead, and you should be, but never fear – we're about to share all our coping mechanisms and tools with you. Honestly. We promise. You're Grand.

3

GRAND BASICS

(A Starter Pack)

★

Some of you readers weren't born Irish women. Don't be too hard on yourselves; we can't all be instinctively Grand. That's totally OK. We can all do more to be the best Irish women we can be. You just need a few basics to get you started.

Everyone seems to have an opinion on Irish women and what makes us tick. But there's a lot going on beneath these jumpers and shawls. You think you know us, but you don't. We have wants. We have needs. Here, we explore those in a little more detail.

How To Be an Irishwoman: Starter Pack

•••••

1. Don't put up with any nonsense. This doesn't necessarily mean you deal directly with every

issue – or even any issue – you come across, but you should definitely moan loudly about it later.

2. Talk about the weather all the time, but never be equipped for what it's actually doing right at that moment. That'd be much too straightforward. You're going for complexity here. As mentioned earlier, being contrary is our stock in trade.

3. Do things "against all odds". Because there are a lot of odds against you, so you might as well do the things anyway.

4. Be fierce. Not in an *America's Next Top Model* kind of way (although we are pretty expert at stomping). Our wrath is mighty: an Irishwoman can wither anything or anyone with just a look. Use this power wisely.

5. Drink tea (sometimes called "tay"). We can and will debunk certain stereotypes, but this one is true. There is nothing that can't be made better with tea.

6. Know very little about your family's heritage. There's just too much. It'd weigh you down. Leave it to your foreign cousins – it'll give you something to talk about when they come over.

7. Carry a map of Ireland with you everywhere

you go. You need to be acutely aware of
where you come from – literally and
figuratively – and where you're going. Even
if there isn't any wifi.

8. Be a fast walker. We are, apparently, the
fastest in Europe. Aim to beat the hair-frizzing
moisture in the air by staying a few paces
ahead of it.

Cottage Industry Alerts

. . . . .

Ireland has a lot of cottages. They're where we had our ideas, as
well as our tea. Now, yet again, times are hard and we could all
use a bit of extra cash. So we're going to give you some business
ideas throughout the book. They won't always be the obvious,
for instance goats have been done to death. These will be a little
different. So keep your eyes peeled for our Cottage Industry
Alerts: there's nothing an Irishwoman can't make money out of
if she tries.

Grand Stereotypes/ Not So Grand Stereotypes

·····

Everyone loves a bit of mystique, and no one more so than Irish women. We pride ourselves on being difficult to figure out. It's all those years of hiding from the Vikings/English/TV licence inspector: we see every social interaction as a possible interrogation and we don't want to give too much away. Clichés and generalisations are our mortal enemies: when you're talking about us in general terms, you have to be very, very careful. Erupting volcano careful.

There are thousands of clichés about the Irish so it might be tricky to tell which stereotypes we enjoy and which we don't, but it's not impossible. For example, nobody minds being compared to Maureen O'Hara in *The Quiet Man*. All wild and strong and catching the eye of an American: that doesn't suck. But in case common sense fails, here's a list to help you through the minefield.

STEREOTYPES WE LIKE	STEREOTYPES WE DON'T LIKE
We all like potatoes. We may hate to admit it, but that one is true.	We're all farmers. All that fresh air and communing with nature? We wish.
Maureen O'Hara.	St Bridget.
We're all superstitious (touch wood).	We're all religious.
We're a bit thick (useful disguise for eavesdropping/ info gathering).	We're a bit thick. Feck off, now.
We're feisty and take no nonsense.	We'd hit you a dig as soon as look at you.
We're great with words.	We're bad at sums.
We're very welcoming.	We're doormats .
We're "handsome", or "comely".	We all have red hair.
We're not backwards about coming forward.	Don't mind me, I'll just sit here in the dark.
We're a bit magical-mystical.	We're drunk.
We're a bit wild.	We're ever-pregnant.
We're never far from the teapot	We're always in the pub

TARA FLYNN

Grand Role Models

•••••

While we're on the subject of how we're perceived, there are of course certain women we've traditionally been encouraged to be like. But the ones we're supposed to hold in high esteem can be quite different to the ones we Modern Irish Women really like.

WHO WE'RE MEANT TO ADMIRE	WHO WE REALLY ADMIRE
The Blessed Virgin Mary	The Commitmentettes
St. Bridget	The President Marys
Peig	The Dunnes Stores Strikers
Dana	Katie Taylor
	The Condom Train Women
	The Invisible Women
	Camogie players
	The Ireland Women's Rugby team
	Anne Doyle
	Sinéad O'Connor
	Panti Bliss
	Female politicians who put up with late-night bum-pats
Mammy	Mammy

iMOM:
Irish Mother or Mammy

•••••

Ah, here she is! We've met her briefly already, but as you may have guessed from every book written about Ireland ever, she's incredibly significant.

The classic iMOM (Irish Mother or Mammy) is an icon: a stout, selfless, hardy woman with rosy cheeks, dressed either in an apron or her Mass coat, flour ever on her hands, child ever on her hip. Dispenser of advice, kisser of boo-boos. cook, nurse, stretcher of fivers, spoiler of sons.

"Mammy", as she's better known, has been celebrated and feared in song, story and legend all over the world. There's not much more to add. Irish mammies are beloved and we wouldn't be where we are today without them.

They're also modern women, though, so that's why we've brought mammy up to date with a new acronym – iMOM (Irish Mother or Mammy).

iMOM might sound a bit like a robot, but sure aren't mammies programmed to do everything for us? (For their sons, anyway?)

iMOM

• • • • •

★ She stores all your data (all of it – including bad memories and photos you'd rather had been destroyed).

★ She reminds you of important dates (like the month's mind of that relative you never met).

★ She's full of songs and stories. You'll never be bored with an iMOM around.

★ She produces the food she knows you like, on plates exactly the right temperature, like the computer in *Star Trek*.

★ But unlike her techno counterparts, the iMOM has a very long battery life and is completely waterproof.

WE HEART iMOM.

Non-iMOM

•••••

In the eyes of the world, all Irish women are programmed to be iMOMs. Traditionally, it was pretty much the only job open to women. Even after 2 different Marys headed the country for 28 years between them, being an iMOM is still – in many circles – held as the pinnacle of an Irishwoman's achievement.

If you're not an iMOM, I'm sorry, but you're just not taking this seriously enough. You're letting the side down. And while it's true that society the world over puts pressure on women to procreate, women in other countries don't have the icon that is iMOM to live up to.

If you're an Irishwoman and you've chosen to be child-free – WHY? You want to be a rudderless ship, drifting aimlessly through life from selfish smoothie to selfish massage to selfish sun holiday (as it's assumed child-free people do)? You probably don't even pay your taxes and you'd never help old ladies across the street or put out a fire. Seriously, in the face of attitudes like this, it really might just be easier to reproduce.

Childless, it will be much more difficult to reach iconic status in Ireland, so let's attempt to debunk some of the preconceptions:

NON-iMOM PERCEPTION	NON-iMOM REALITY
You hate children.	You only hate children when they're running around restaurants, "delightfully" throwing spaghetti sauce.
You eat babies, willy-nilly.	It's not willy-nilly. How are the babies done?
You can get pregnant but won't? You're wasting your go.	This isn't Monopoly.
You're letting your partner down.	Screw them and the rest of society. Think of the lie-ins!
You're not fulfilling your ultimate purpose.	Your ultimate purpose is to finish all the box sets. You're getting close.
You only have sex for pleasure and intimacy.	Yup.
You have all the sex, all the time.	You're just one woman.
You're shameless.	You're Irish. Not possible.
You're some kind of riddle.	The answer is "a river".

iMOMs are great. But we can't all be great. Some of us are happy just to be Grand ... so long as we can have the odd selfish smoothie.

••••• ★ •••••

COTTAGE INDUSTRY ALERT: 100% cotton "Non iMOMs are people, too" t-shirts. To be worn ironically, obviously.

••••• ★ •••••

Spiritually Grand: Staying Pagan

•••••

The Catholic Church got Irish women. It got us good. In ancient times we were happy, sex-positive pagans. Far from being ungodly, we had loads of gods, many of them female. And those goddesses were powerful AND hot. They were all about fertility, empowerment, magic and good craic. The menstrual and birth cycles were seen as great miracles. No wonder men were in awe.

One of our best pre-Christian goddesses was Brighid, goddess of light, smithery and all kinds of other good stuff. There was really nothing she couldn't do. She even had a magic cloak thousands of years before Harry Potter.

Then Saint Patrick arrived and waved a shamrock at us, that one wave of a tiny plant giving us both organised religion and the world's lamest emblem. And there's no point saying there's no historical evidence St Pat ever existed because it's too late now. We're Catholics, even those of us who aren't. Perhaps it was the lure of the parades.

Catholicism cleverly swallowed goddesses like Brighid up and made them saints: St Bridget, in this case, who – while she kept her awesome cloak – now answered to God as opposed to being a god herself. (One of St Bridget's miracles was apparently lifting an unwanted pregnancy from a young nun who'd become pregnant and returning her to health, but we don't talk about that now.) Enjoying sex was promptly taken off the table, and practically every other surface, too.

It was the first widespread shushing of Irish women. But in truth, none of the underlying pagan stuff went away. The reason such a no-bullshit people is still so superstitious is the pagan in us, holding on for dear life. We leave doors open on Hallowe'en to let spirits pass through, and we don't pick blackberries after November 1 in case the Púca has spat on them. Early Irish Christians agreed to worship in churches, but built pagan symbols like the Sheela na Gig (a wild, squatting woman, private parts proudly displayed) into them. She was soon discontinued – the Church, as we know, doesn't have much truck with vaginas.

Once Sheela, Brighid and other reminders of our paganism went, it seems we overcompensated and became the best, most judgemental, miserable Christians we could be. What were our indigenous beliefs compared to the magic of eternal life? Which, of course, wasn't magic. It was real. A tiny plant told us so.

Grand Politics

• • • • •

Politics run deep in the Irish psyche, so we have to go into them a bit. Party politics can be a bit boring, we know, so we'll keep it brief.

The thing to do is to really dig deep into your contrary nature: pick a stance and defend it, even if you're contradicting yourself from five minutes ago. This goes both for our elected representatives and for every pub politician up and down the country. Politicians worldwide lie – sorry, "put spin on the facts" – but in Ireland, there's a full-on art to saying loads while saying nothing at all. No wonder Ronan Keating had a hit with that song that time.

You can look up Ireland's main political parties if you like, but the main thing to keep in mind is that they are all exactly the same. They even recycle each other's campaign slogans. It wouldn't surprise me if they wore each other's clothes sometimes, just to mix things up and confuse us all further.

There's something endearing about their shenanigans. It's kind of cute when someone tries to lie but can't get away with it, like they're 8. You just want to ruffle their hair and congratulate them for taking the time to try.

There's a sudden upsurge of female politicians in Ireland. Finally! It's as if someone's realised that the Grand future of the country's women probably isn't only in the kitchen. Maybe they'll be able to address the issues that even the UN has with how women have been dealt with here. It'll be a shame if they don't. But either way, there's more representation for us now. In old Ireland, there was a mistrust for the callous, half-women who had children and then returned to work or – worse – chose not to have children at all. That would have been just the kind of person who'd go into politics, the very kind of ambitious go-getter this country did not want at its helm, changing stuff. No wonder it took women a while to get elected.

Ambition was not to be trusted. Or, at any rate, it was to be trusted far less than lies. At least with lies, you knew where you stood. So the country may not know itself with so many women candidates, but we have a little way to go on our political journey yet. And there's one small symbolic problem. You can't spell "Dáil" without "Lad".

····★·····

"LAPGATE"

During a long and heated debate on abortion legislation in the Dáil in 2013, a male TD pulled a female colleague onto his lap and tried to give her a bit of a cuddle. That's right. During a parliamentary session.

People were quick to criticise, dubbing the incident "Lapgate" and saying it was absurdly sexist and inappropriate, particularly given the gravity of the subject under discussion.

But guys, maybe we're being too harsh. What if he was offering the deputy some much-needed cuddly solidarity? Granted, it looked like a weird, late-night bar-room scene; but did anyone stop to think that he might have just been dragging her onto his lap the better to whisper support for women's rights into her ear? No? Well, just in case that happened (and it didn't), let's not be so quick to judge.

Female politicians worldwide can only dream of such Grand hands-on support. Except maybe in Italy.

•••••★•••••

Now all that's left for you to do is vote.

•••••★•••••

HOW TO VOTE:

★ Do you know the candidate from the pub? Do they cheat at cards? If so, vote for them. That's the kind of initiative we need in government.

★ Did the candidate's granddad and your granddad used to hang out? If yes, vote for them. Don't even question it; it's a thing.

★ Does the candidate have a nice poster? If so, don't vote for them. They've too much free time to be messing about on Photoshop.

It ultimately doesn't matter: they really are all the same. So just take pot luck and enjoy the outcome! The country will be Grand!

Being Reared Far from Something

•••••

In the "tall poppy" tradition we love so much in Ireland, people won't be long letting you know if you're being insincere. Like if you're wearing too much perfume, or sunglasses. You will be cut down to size, called out immediately, and while you might not be cursed from a height* (*see Casting a Curse from a Height), there will be some form of public denouncing or ridicule. You will be told in a loud voice for all to hear that "'Tis far from X you were reared."

••••• ★ •••••

EXAMPLE:

Facebook post: *Here's a picture of me at the Taj Mahal! #indiatrip*
Comments 1 – 78: *'Tis far from the Taj Mahal you were reared.*
Comment 79: *You lucky thing. Looking great!**
Comments 80 – 100: *'Tis far from the Taj Mahal you were reared.*
In other words: "Who do you think you are, rubbing your Taj Mahal in our stuck-in-

Ireland faces? You probably think you're great."

*Comment 79 will have been left by an American cousin.

• • • • • ★ • • • • •

'Tis far from X you were reared" is damning, and it's meant to be. Which is great, because rather than wholeheartedly enjoy something and lose the run of yourself, which you do not want to do, you'll be put back in your place lickety split.

There are certain things that it will be assumed that every Irishwoman was reared far from.

(NB actual geographical distance of rearing from entity is irrelevant):

- ★ Avocados
- ★ Quail
- ★ Symphonies
- ★ Mani Pedis
- ★ Fluency in another language
- ★ Paris. Even if you were reared there.
- ★ Trail mix. What's wrong with Tayto?
- ★ Cricket
- ★ Eau de Cologne
- ★ Hobnobs (biscuits)
- ★ The Blackrock Clinic
- ★ HBO

★ Water features
★ Any jam other than "marmalade jam" or "red"
★ Thank You cards
★ Goujons
★ Contraceptives
★ After-dinner mints
★ Underfloor heating
★ Bagels, or any other kind of bread that doesn't come loaf-shaped

Any or all of the above may be perfectly commonplace where you are. It doesn't matter. You must pretend you've never heard of or done any of them. And if anyone else should bring them up, now – after hooting with derision and rolling your eyes – you know what to say.

You Think You're Great

•••••

As you've seen, if something good happens, it's best to pretend it hasn't. It's Grand you're after: good is too much. Even buying a ripe avocado might be perceived as bragging. But why? You see, every Irish girl has been trained not to lose the run of herself. She's raised to be diligent, hard-working and even try to do well, but never to believe she's got there.

You might say that Irish women have the lowest self-esteem

in the world, but you'd have to quickly retract that in case someone thought you were boasting. "We're the best at thinking the worst of ourselves." No! We're the worst. Just the worst.

The most damning thing you could say to an Irish child is "You think you're great." Oh, that hurts. That cuts to the quick.

In American TV shows, parents, teachers, guardian angels and cat-eating aliens were forever telling kids that they *were* great. "Believe in yourself. You can do it!" But that wouldn't wash here. Not in Ireland.

Here, if someone says that you think you're great, you must immediately attempt to set them straight. "I don't! I don't think I'm great! I'm awful. I have appallingly low self-esteem!"

This level of one-downmanship is difficult to shake off. On the upside, it's the reason we don't have the smell of ourselves.

How to Take a Compliment

• • • • •

This technically isn't a secret: every comedian, columnist and commentator has observed the following phenomenon, but it's so prevalent that it can't be left out.

How to take a compliment: DON'T. You mustn't. You are an Irishwoman and have far more important things going on than to be taking notice of idle flattery. Looks aren't nearly as important as whatever you're doing – managing a company, organising a protest or – preferably – giving birth. At least,

that's what you have to make everyone think.

Compliments are lovely and Irish women are just as susceptible to them as everyone else. But way more valuable here than looking good or being praised for something is not having a big head. You do not want anyone to think you think you're great.

How NOT to handle a compliment:

A: "That's a nice lipstick. It really suits you."
B: "Oh, thank you. Yes, I like it too."
Silence.
A: (under breath) "Bitch."

This is how that should have gone:

A: "That's a nice lipstick. It really suits you."
B: "Feck off. Are you messing?"
A: "No! It's lovely."
B: "No … Stop … It's shite. I wish the lights would fail."
A: "Ah, you look great. Where did you get it?"
B: "God, I'm not sure. Can't remember. I think I fished it out of a sewer I was passing, YEARS ago. Then this morning I couldn't find my contacts so I grabbed the nearest thing and put it on in the dark without looking. It's shite, isn't it? Do I look like an eejit?"
A: "No, seriously. You look great. Learn to take a compliment, would you!"

You both laugh.

And that, right there, is the ultimate Irish compliment. You bat away an actual compliment so long, it looks as if you haven't even noticed it. You just had so much else on your mind. You don't have a big head! So you get the original praise, with the glow of knowing that you're perceived as humble, deep and just effortlessly beautiful on top of it all. Who wouldn't love that?

• • • • • ★ • • • • •

I GOT IT IN PENNEYS

When it comes to clothes, compliments must be responded to with a stock answer: "I got it in Penneys."*

It doesn't matter if it was custom made for you by an Italian in an atelier and you flew out to Milan for three fittings to get it just right before carefully choosing this moment to share it with the rest of the world and wear it into town: *you got it in Penneys.*

This shows

(a) you're not clothes obsessed, you just throw on clothes while thinking about the previously mentioned other important stuff.

(b) you're so fashion forward, you can rock

something that only cost €3-for-two. You're so down to earth, you shop where everyone else shops – where they have a whole lotta things for Christmas – and make it look good. You're not above your station. We are all in the same club. You got it in Penneys.

Got that? Great. And where did you get it? *Penneys*. Good. At least we've sorted that one out.

*Other shops are available. Like Dunnes, or Shaws: Almost Nationwide.

····· ★ ·····

Giving Someone the Soot

·····

Irish women are very generous. But if someone isn't deemed to be deserving, the one thing we will never give them is the soot. This soot isn't found up a chimney, but in phrases like "I wouldn't give them the soot of it", meaning "I don't want them to know they've had an effect on me, or that I even realise they exist at all."

It's usually applied to someone who has wronged an Irishwoman in some way. For instance, you would never give an ex who dumped you by text the soot of anything ever again. Here it is in a few more contexts, just so it's clear.

•••••★•••••

He said he wasn't ready for a relationship, then he walked in with an 8-foot blonde fiancée. But I *didn't give him the soot* of letting him know I saw them. I just kept on playing *Twister*.

I didn't tell her she was right about this hair colour not suiting me. I *wouldn't give her the soot* of it. Now, please pass me my hat.

That American tourist knew more about Christ Church than I did, but he was such a know-it-all, I made up some new "facts" to throw him. I just couldn't *give him the soot* of being better informed about Ireland than me.

•••••★•••••

Tea: Grand Elixir of Life Hot Topic and Hot Drop

•••••

Every woman needs a little help in the quest for being Grand. Exhausted from surviving, batting away compliments, and battling boldness, we need all the fuel we can get. And what

Irish women run on is mainly tea. Reams have been written on how to make the perfect cup of tea, or "tay". It is drunk in the scientific quantities of pots, cups and drops. It can be a touchy political subject:

★ milk in first or second
★ milk in at all
★ sugar or something fancy like lemon
  (if you've just come back from abroad)
★ leaf or bag, let alone …
★ brand. Don't even go there. Like politics, it's best not to discuss tea at all when you're away from your immediate family: chances are they do things differently around here and you don't want to alienate someone forever over the very potion that might bring you together.

We may no longer be goddesses or druids, but that doesn't mean we don't have a magical elixir that makes everything OK. No wonder we drink more "tay" per capita than almost anywhere else on the planet. We need it. And it works. If only they'd had more tea on battlefields down through the years, a lot less blood might have been spilt on this land. It'd have been milk that flowed instead. If only we could agree when it went in.

PROBLEMS TEA CAN MAKE GRAND	PROBLEMS TEA CAN'T MAKE GRAND
Heartbreak	Disagreements about how to make tea
Ageing	
Loneliness	
Boredom	
Menstrual cramps	
Hot-headedness	
Lethargy	
Hangovers	
Lack of conversation	
Homesickness	
Thirst	

COTTAGE INDUSTRY ALERT: Roadside tea stands. Anywhere. Everywhere. You'll make a fortune and lifelong friends.

The Essions

·····

We have so many reasons for needing tea, magical tea. Not least that by the time she hits her teens, every Irishwoman will probably have encountered at least one of the Essions, possibly several times. Depression, oppression, suppression, repression, confession – any of them really, none of them is good. Luckily, in Ireland, women have a great way of countering these grim Essions with an Ession of our own: the sEssion. Nothing like a gigantic gathering of foot tapping, knee slapping, spoon playing pals to sing the oppression away.

And tea. Pots and pots of tea.

How To Spot an Irishwoman at a Distance

·····

It's easy to tell an Irishwoman once you get talking to her. The accent, the attitude, the feisty approach to tea-making. But how do you know if you're dealing with an Irishwoman before it's too late?

IN GENERAL: Forget the red hair and sturdy ankles nonsense, you will instantly

recognise an Irishwoman by her strong shoulders. This comes from years of standing tall against oppression, shame and strong winds. Also from numerous attempts to swim off the island. Our shoulders are a dead giveaway. (See also Hibernomorph in A Grand Pair of Genes.)

ACTUALYJJJSSS: The Irishwoman is of course the one making like a bag of ferrets under a beach towel, and having a picnic in her car. (See also How to be a Ferret in Nudity.)

AT THE PUB: She's the one decisively ordering a pint. Because in the (fairly recent) past, she couldn't, but now, she can.

AT THE AIRPORT: She's either the one wearing a green uniform welcoming you onto a plane to New York, or she's the one crying in her seat because she's (a) leaving Ireland or (b) going back.

IN ROME: She's the one who heads straight to the Vatican, but then stands in the middle of St Peter's, conflicted, wondering what the feck she's doing there. She finds an Irish pub instead.

AT A MARCH: Irish women have to take to the streets so often, protesting all kinds of

injustice, that we've become very good at it. If you see a march anywhere in the world, assume Irish women are somehow involved. Especially in Ireland.

AT A ST PATRICK'S DAY PARADE:
You are unlikely to spot any Irish women at St Patrick's Day events, anywhere. The floppy felt buckle hat craze simply never took off here. We were far too oppressed for floppy felt.

Beware of imposters. You have been warned.

Grand Names

•••••

Now that you're able to spot us, what exactly are we called? Well, I have one bit of sad news, Americans: it's not Colleen. Colleen is not a name. Sorry if it's your name. But Colleen isn't a name. Colleen is the Anglicised spelling of the Irish for girl: *cailín*.

••••• ★ •••••

MADE UP FACT #1

As we saw in Peig, where most girls are called Cáit, the Irish were too busy trying not to die from hunger and the like to be thinking of names for the girl children. Sure, apart from the odd Mass, girls would never be out of the house for long and no one would need to call them for any reason.

Eventually, they would have their own children and by that time, be known as "mammy". So the boys were called Seán and Mick and Séamas, and the girls were called "girl" – Colleen. And that's why almost all Irish-American women are called that. Name, function and job description. What more would you want?

● ● ● ● ● ★ ● ● ● ● ●

But the Colleens of this world are the lucky ones. Irish girls' names are awful. Just awful. You took your pick from tragic heroine, fake saint, mound, or sound resembling someone choking on an old sock. *Gráinne*, the name with the most beautiful meaning – *love* (shared with a mythological heroine and a really fierce pirate) – sounds like you're starting a fight. Maybe Granuaile (Grace O'Malley) became a pirate by accident; she just introduced herself and people got the wrong idea and drew their swords. She then had no choice but to fight back.

Ah, Feck: The Next Generation (Ex-Pats)

· · · · ·

Now that we're talking about our American cousins, let's visit with them for a while. That's right, descendants of ex-pats, I'm talking about you.

When is an Irishwoman not an Irishwoman? When she's never even been to Ireland – but she does not let that stop her being the most fervently, passionately, annoyingly Irish version of an Irishwoman she can be. With, to be fair, a fair whack of the good stuff too.

Our North American cousins tend to be kind, decent, high-achieving people. They wrote and told us of a wonderland called McDonald's where the chips came in an envelope, and they sent money home. We have a lot to thank them for.

There is no escaping the fact that second-generation Irish know a lot more about Ireland than those of us born here. Don't even TRY and argue. They can recite generations of names and birth, baptism, marriage and death dates of every family member you never knew you had.

But their view freezes at whatever period the last native left. They think the Church in Ireland still has a deep universal influence; if only they knew loads of us had been ducking out of Mass for years. They think we still have donkeys, when we've

WHAT THEY'VE BEEN TOLD

We all go to Mass, and miss Pope Benedict.

We live in thatched cottages.

Pigs in the kitchen.

Dancing at the crossroads.

Chastity (as if).

We have no amenities.

Jay-Z put us on the map.

We all have massive families.

We celebrate St Patty's Day.

Our national emblem is a lucky four-leaf clover.

We had a "Potato Famine".

YOU'RE GRAND

3

WHAT IT'S LIKE NOW

We go for brunch, and order Eggs Benedict.
We'll pitch you a cottage industry idea.
Bacon curing as part of said cottage industry idea.
We're only just in from the office. No time.
Riding. Swearing.
We had mobile phones before you were born.
Google did that.
We've had contraception for a while now.
It's St Patrick. Or Paddy. Patty's a mint.
It's a shamrock. Three leaves. And no luck.
It's called "The Famine". "The Great Famine",
if you're feeling positive about it. There was
NO OTHER FOOD AVAILABLE. *Potato*
Famine makes us sound picky, like we were
turning down banquets, holding out for spuds.
You might as well list all the other things we
didn't have while you're at it: pasta famine,
quail famine, Flaked Salmon Soufflé famine.
We didn't have any of those either. Besides,
there's no record of any potatoes starving
or emigrating. So please stop saying Potato
Famine. Thanks.

had buses for ages. That we have to have spuds with every meal … well, that one is true.

Ireland has changed since Great-Great-Great-Granddad sailed to Canada, and many of those changes have been positive. Not all, obviously. We're nowhere near as welcoming as they've been taught to believe by older relatives with shamrock-coloured glasses. Our foreign cousins often get a shock when they arrive at Busáras and have their pocket picked. *Fáilte!*

Grand Talkers

• • • • •

We couldn't leave our worst-kept secret out of your starter pack: we're great talkers. Well spotted. We're almost as good, if not better, at the talking as the walking (which we'll come back to). Every year, thousands of people kiss a weird, lipstick covered slab on top of a castle in Blarney in the hopes of getting some of our Gift of the Gab.

But you don't need to kiss any slabs. You just need to open your mouth. The main thing is to never, ever skimp on the details. Let's say you've just been to the shop, and you saw Áine. You could just say, "I went to the shop and I saw Áine." But that would be a waste of a Grand conversational opportunity. You must include at least some of the following:

• • • • • ★ • • • • •

THE ART OF GRAND CONVERSATION

Open with "Grand day for it, all the same."
Never discuss what "it" is.

Then move – slowly – on to:

Where you've just come from.
What happened there.
You'll never guess who was there.
Where they were standing.
Why they were there.
What they were wearing.
The state of the country.
What direction the wind was coming from.
Who they vote for.
Who their father was.
Any other relevant relatives.
Some less relevant relatives.
Random non-sequiturs.
The goverment are a pile of goballoons, or
   shower of them.
Whether or not you have a touch of indigestion/
   heartburn/gout.
Who was trying to eavesdrop.
Was it raining? (It was. You still can't leave
   this out.)

Who's died (there's always someone).
How you feel about all of the above.
Something about the Joe Duffy show.
How the other party might have felt.
Forget logic.
Embellish.
Try singing some of it.

The only thing to watch out for is that you never know who's listening. There's a strong possibility she's the sister of whomever you're discussing. Try saying any names out of the side of your mouth, directly at your intended listener. This won't save you in all cases, but it does help.

You've seen how many words Joyce used in Ulysses? That's an Irish fella being concise. And there's proof that women are more verbal than men, using more descriptive words and more words in general – probably making up for lost time after all the years of shushing. So get your thesaurus out and get yapping. And don't you ever stop.

City Mouse, Culchie Mouse

•••••

With so many people squishing us, telling us what we shouldn't be doing, it'd be nice to say that Irish women always have each other's backs. And in general, we do. But there is one last great

divide we can't get past, try as we might: the gap between "townie" and "culchie".

A "culchie" is someone from the countryside, or small town. Or just plain outside Dublin. In fact, Dubliners are really the only people in the land who will never be called culchies at some point. You're either a townie or a culchie and there's nothing you can do about it.

The origin of the word "culchie" is sketchy, but it's most likely onomatopoeic – like the "squelchy" muck from which we're believed to come.

We're supposed to be un-chic, good with animals, able to predict the weather, have few electrical outlets and be very friendly, but a biteen thick. City dwellers tend to see themselves as having attributes exactly the opposite of these. In other words, they think they're great.

There was an attempt to give Dubs the nickname "Jackeen" but it doesn't seem to sting as much as "culchie" does. In fact, they like it because it makes them feel even more Dubliny. We've even tried to take back "culchie" for ourselves, but the lingering bovine associations just can't quite be shaken off. Still, culchie is infinitely better than some of the other country names: mucker, bogger, mulshie, sheep shagger, bogwoman, muck savage and hundreds of other things we probably don't get called to our faces.

We'd like to propose some more positive alternatives for

rural Irish women: Silage Surfers, Turf Gurrrls, Muck Gliders, Bog Managers, Farm Fresh, Queens of the Stone Walls, Earth Angels or Churn Ups.

We're just not sure they'll be allowed to catch on.

Casting a Curse from a Height

• • • • •

In Ancient Times, druids (a kind of magical rock star) used to go up hills when required and curse someone – literally – from a height. If you'd been wronged, made to feel less than Grand, you didn't sue the wrongdoer, you gave the druid some hiking boots, a packed lunch and a map to the nearest mountain. Off up it he'd go to fling a curse in the direction of the wrongdoer. The magic was somehow stronger with the weight of gravity behind it ... look, we're not really sure how it worked but it did because it's something we still say today: "I cursed him from a height." After years learning from the magical pros, Irish women have cursing down to a fine art.

We seem pretty laid back, but you DO NOT want to cross us. You should try not to be on the receiving end of a curse if you can manage it. They may look and sound like "just words" but pair curses with a dirty look and all that gravity and

BOOM – milk goes sour, or cars conk out completely. These may be purely coincidental – milk goes off all by itself and cars are notorious bastards – but the fact that we feel like we had something to do with the process makes us feel so much better.

In myth, Gráinne threatened Diarmaid with "the pain of a woman in childbirth", if he wouldn't run away with her. He was a big old warrior but he ran away with her. Sure, she was hot, but it was knowing that curses can come true that clinched the deal. (It's said that they never had fresh milk in the house.)

The simplest curse is "May they have no luck." If someone's been mugged or burgled, it's comforting. Because you know it works. Even if you never really have anything to do with the eventual toe-stubbing, you feel like you did. And that's a great feeling. Karma may be a bitch, but it has nothing on an Irishwoman scorned.

●●●●● ★ ●●●●●

COTTAGE INDUSTRY ALERT: Outside of solstices, druids aren't as visible as they previously were. Nothing to stop you offering an urban curse from a height service (for a nominal fee). It'd also be a great use for all those disused cranes, until the next fictitious property boom.

Here are some curse ideas to get you started:

May your drains be as blocked as your bowels.
May your ex be in the supermarket and you
  there in your pyjamas.
May the wax dry too fast for the waxing strip.
May the Guards and none hear of your lock-in,
  unless none of them be already in attendance.
May Daniel O'Donnell sing at your funeral.
May your single chart only in Denmark.
May the road rise to meet you in the face.

• • • • • ★ • • • • •

Love/Hate: Trust Issues

• • • • •

To say that Irish women are contrary or self-contradictory is putting it mildly. We're good, but we're bold. We love Ireland, but we'll be the first to say "what a kip". We build each other up and cut each other down just as quickly. We bitch about our families, but you had better not. We are both the greatest secret keepers and the finest gossips. Misery makes us happy.

We share a tragic history, so we love the craic. What we know as "realism" is really "pessimistic optimism". Basically, like our weather, we're delightfully fickle. You could justifiably say that we don't know our arse from our elbow. It can be hard to know who you can trust.

A great west Cork compliment is "You could tell her the killing of a man", meaning "she'd keep your confession of murder to herself". That's a lot of trust. Though the dead person doesn't benefit from it. If I were the dead person, I'd want anyone hearing the news to at least call the cops, if not immediately set about avenging my death. But you'd never tell. Unless it made a good story.

So, here's my advice: you can safely put all your trust in an Irishwoman. Just don't leave the room for too long. And don't give her good reason to curse you from a height.

Grand Virtues/Grand Vices

• • • • •

TRADITIONAL IRISH VIRTUES	ACTUAL IRISH VIRTUES
Being a great singer	Not starting a sing-song in the first place
Chastity	Discretion
A great devotion to Our Lady	Not shoving personal beliefs at anyone else
Sewing your own clothes	Getting it in Penneys
Being an iMOM	Distracting people from your non-iMOM status by getting tea into them, fast

TRADITIONAL IRISH VICES	ACTUAL IRISH VICES
Stealing	Getting caught stealing
Missing confession	Missing the *Late Late* Toy Show
Not getting your round in	Not getting your round in
Arriving with your hands hanging to you (not bringing a gift when you visit)	Forgetting to arrive at all – we didn't really mean it when we asked you to drop in
Moving to England	Being happy about moving to England
Laziness	Wasting a hard-earned lie-in
Not being an iMOM	Not being fast enough with the offer of tea

4

KNOWING
YOUR
PLACE

★

Irish women face a daily dilemma: we know our natural home is in the kitchen, being an iMOM. At least, that's where the hardened traditionalists would like us to be. But we've changed. It's 2014. Bills need to be paid. The tug between a traditional view of Irish women and who we really are now has never been greater. Sometimes, you have to fake it til you make it and keep the traditionalists out of your hair. For a while, anyway.

Just remember what all Irish women know: <u>you can't have it all</u>, so don't be attempting to. You'll only be even more disappointed than you already are. Know your place, whether in the house or out of it, and you'll be Grand.

How To Know Your Place
• • • • •

Of course, it goes without saying that no matter how good a girl you may seem, your inner bold streak won't have gone anywhere.

But sometimes you have to give 'em what they think they want. Basically, if you answer "No" to the following questions, you know your place, like a good girl. Congratulations. If not, it might be time to start getting into practice.

••••• ★ •••••

QUESTIONS YOU SHOULD BE ANSWERING "NO" TO

Is anyone scowling at you?

Are you in prison?

Are you "going to England" or planning to do so?

Are you protesting against anything right now?

Has anyone in the last week referred to you as uppity, loud, strident, or being possessed of a "strong personality"? Or just plain old "possessed"?

Are you currently stifling burning rage at some injustice or other?

Have you publicly disagreed with a lobby group with plenty of financial backing?

••••• ★ •••••

If you answered "Yes" to any of the above, tread carefully. You seem to have an extra bold streak which will make you the envy of all of us. But we might just have to keep an eye on you.

Things To Do "Like a Good Girl"

• • • • •

You never have to wonder how a good girl should act if you live in Ireland, because you'll be told all the time:

"Keep quiet, like a good girl."

"Put the kettle on, like a good girl."

"Don't be worrying yourself with those complex thoughts, like a good girl."

"Bring the turf in, like a good girl."

"Enter the National Song Contest, like a good girl."

"Go to England, like a good girl."

"Off my bar stool, like a good girl."

"Eat that up, like a good girl."

The basic requirements are silence, obedience (real or put on) and invisibility. All that good stuff. Got it? Good.

What you'd never hear anyone asking you to do "like a good girl":

★ Push back boundaries
★ Leave a bit on your plate
★ Think outside the box
★ Become a politician
★ Go to America
★ Take a break for yourself
★ Put on a bit more make-up
★ Turn down that air hostessing job

And, no, you will never, ever hear any bloke aged over 7 being asked to do anything "like a good boy".

How To Be Difficult

•••••

Do anything that suggests you're out of your place, e.g.

★ Query a bill.
★ Make a fuss.
★ Say, "This isn't what we agreed." Pointing facts out is unfeminine.
★ Argue a point. This will of course earn you strident harpie points.
★ Raise your voice. That's not being very quiet like a good girl. What were you thinking?

A Grand Bit O' Dhinner

•••••

Knowing your place can take a lot of energy. You're going to need to make sure you get the right kind of sustenance. Irish women cannot live on tea alone, as magical a potion as it may be.

Irish cuisine could, in the past, have been summed up as "potatoes and a dream". It really was miraculous how it was possible to take incredible local vegetables, almost universal access to fresh seafood, and meat and dairy produce that were the toast of Europe, and condense them all down into a warm, grey sludge. With two different kinds of spuds. (Three if it's a wedding.)

That's all changed in the last couple of decades. There are tons of great chefs and restaurants now, if you can handle the shame of not being the one doing the cooking and resist the urge to help.

But mostly, you won't be able to handle that shame, so you'll be providing meals at home. For an imaginary family if need be: don't think you can skip out just because you're not an iMOM. Oh, no.

Over many centuries, Irish meals have evolved according to the strict guidelines set out below.

NOTE: Irish people don't really like new foods. Best leave the fancy stuff to the chefs.

TARA FLYNN

MADE UP FACT #2

"New foods" means things like fruit. Like *Playboy* magazine, grapes were banned from Ireland until relatively recently on the grounds of being "too suggestive" and "full of pips" (see the great *Playboy* pip scandal of 1978).

You can get all kinds of foods here now, since someone came back from Italy with an espresso machine and notions, but that's not what we're talking about here. We're talking about the food we were raised on by iMOMs, which was good enough for us.

There are three traditional Irish meals. Three meals. That's it. 'Tis far from snacks we were reared. These three meals are:

THE BREAKFAST, THE DHINNER AND THE TAY

Which is the most important meal of the day? All of them, given that you're lucky to have them, and they should be eaten as quickly as possible in case they go away again. Savouring is for fanciful eejits who don't know what side their bread is buttered on, wasting their time appreciating the freshness of the butter

instead of getting the bread down them before it's wrenched out of their hands by God/fate/an opportunistic seagull.

••••• ★ •••••

THE BREAKFAST:

EVERY DAY: A big bowl of porridge that sticks to the spoon and the pot and your ribs. Usually made with milk. What kind? There is only one kind: milk, straight from the cow to your bowl.

SUNDAYS/SPECIAL DAYS: A fry. What tourists call "the full Irish", i.e. anything you can fit into a smoking hot oily pan. Preferably pig-related, but fry everything. *Do not toast the bread. Fry it.* Tell visiting children not to slow down too much in the kitchen: they'll be fried.

(On the off chance someone wasn't feeling well enough for the fry, they were allowed special dispensation to just have brown bread and jam [red jam or marmalade jam]. But to get out of a fry, you'd really have to have a doctor's note, or at least prove you had a temperature.)
You can drink whatever you like with The

Breakfast so long as it's a:

GRAND MUG OF TAY

No water, no juice, no crying.

This first meal of the day will carry you through to the next important meal of the day, which happens in "the evening" (12.01pm to 6pm). This meal is known as

THE DHINNER:

Commonly known as "the bit o' dhinner". As in "Did you get the bit o' dhinner?" or "Will you not stay for the bit o' dhinner?" It's important not to let on how much of The Dhinner you ate or plan to eat. So for discussion purposes, dhinner is measured in "bits" only.

But it'd be safe to assume it were a full-on dhinner. The kind of dhinner you'd offer to a visiting dignitary or priest. Spuds, cabbage, and some kind of salty meat, lovingly drowned in a sauce more flour than anything, with green bits in on special occasions.

Dessert (known as "sweet", never "pudding" – pudding is for The Breakfast, or The

Christmas, or for when you're trying to impress someone from The London). "Sweet" was hot and lumpy and yellow-flavoured, with an optional dollop of red jam on top.

Afterwards, say "That was a grand bit o' dhinner", unless you were the cook. In which case, say nothing: you don't think you're great, after all.

GRAND MUG OF TAY

No one ever admitted to it, but no one liked Sweet. It was fecking horrible. But also, they were saving their sweet-tooths and palates for the big one:

THE TAY:

The Tay is Irish teatime. There'll be no cocked pinkie fingers here and nothing will come in tiers. But there will be cake. Cake is the cornerstone of The Tay. There might be some sort of nod to a real mealtime, savoury "Sangwedges" (sandwiches) or some soup, but cake was the point: breads that were really cakes and cakes that were really bricks, pies with thick crusts that were one of your only

sources of fruit for the year. These were the real point of The Tay.

The ensuing carb coma is the main reason we put up with shit telly here. We're too content in digestion to change the channel.

GRAND MUG OF TAY

… before you go to bed, ragin'.

NB: all of the above meals were to be eaten heads down and in silence, save for the ticking of a loud clock or the bonging of the Angelus.

Grand Etiquette

Hundreds of books have been written on etiquette, and how to do things "right". But that's all a bit Graaaahnd. Irish women don't have much truck with that, for the following reasons:

(a) Learning rules is like homework, and who has the time?

(b) If something can be done "right", there's way too much opportunity to get it "wrong". What Irishwoman needs any extra judgement in their lives?

(c) We invented hospitality in the first place (even if a lot

of that was for tourists), so it's probably best everyone else takes their lead from us.

You don't need white gloves or the correct thousand-piece cutlery set to have good manners, you just need to make other people feel comfortable. We are the queens of that. It may turn out that we've been lying to them, but in the moment, we make people feel Grand. Maybe even Grand altogether.

So ditch all those rules about who gets served first, on what side, and how ladies should sit or stand or get in and out of cars. Here's the golden rule of Irish etiquette:

Q: Is everyone having a good time?
A:
> (a) Yes
> (b) No

If you answered (a), congratulations. You will be the hit of the social scene.

If (b), get the rod out of your arse, chill the feck out, have a grand cup of tea for yourself and come back to us when you're ready to have guests.

That polite enough for you?

Note: do say "please" and "thank you" and that basic stuff, though: otherwise, people will think you've lost the run of yourself and talk about you.

Grand Job

· · · · ·

Isn't it great how great women in the workplace have it in Ireland now? It's a wonder our heads don't explode with the power. We might not yet have equal pay or enough childcare to go around but we're out! We can't have it all but we've loads more than we had! Well, some of it! Which is Grand! And we should be grateful!

The lovely old lads who run Ireland from the Dáil and the churches and pubs eventually conceded that Irish women be allowed to work and saw that the bedrock of the country didn't crack and crumble once we started leaving the kitchen for a few hours a day, so long as we promised to come back in time to make The Bit o' Dhinner. Ireland was still Grand. But they don't like us in high-powered jobs. A lady CEO is probably a bit of a bitch; she hasn't known her place for ages.

There are still certain jobs that are best to have if you're an Irishwoman and you don't want to rock the boat. And the Atlantic is very cold. I'd sit down if I were you.

What you want to be is "a credit" to Ireland.

Here are the jobs it's acceptable for an Irishwoman to do.
Women in these professions are a credit to us:

★ Teacher. It's practically an iMOM so this is a
very good job for a woman to have. Preferably
a primary school teacher (85% of primary
teachers here are women); dealing with
young children means you must be maternal
and therefore very good at being a woman
indeed. In fact, teaching is possibly the perfect
Irishwoman job.

★ Air hostess. Not "cabin crew": you are an
air *hostess*. The iMOMs of the sky, in fabulous
green outfits. So like iMOMs, they used to give
out fries even on the short flight to London,
presumably cooked on an Aga in the galley,
with a few hens running around for fresh eggs.
(You don't get these for free anymore, but it's
still part of the training.) Air hostesses are the
last bit of Ireland you'll see before starting
a new life in Boston or somewhere; their
symbolic importance can't be underestimated.
Stern, they could deter a hijacker with just
a look. But they are fair, and the little bit of
sounds-like-Irish they purr into the mic at the

beginning and the end of the flight is a little bit of heaven. I'm sure they'd give you a hug if you asked for it too. They just look that lovely. Not Ryanair, though: they're a no-hugs airline.

★ Singer in the Eurovision.

★ Running your own cottage industry. This not only promotes Ireland but you can do it FROM YOUR KITCHEN and not be taking men's jobs away from them. Ideal.

★ Politician. But only for an approved party and only if you wear big feminine necklaces and avoid talking about "women's issues" too much, causing controversy and wasting Dáil time. An ability to overlook the odd bit of slap and tickle during a parliamentary session will be a great asset to you. Don't lose your sense of humour: take the compliment, Minister Girl!

●●●●●★●●●●●

COTTAGE INDUSTRY ALERT: Make big feminine necklaces out of rocks or recycled materials and sell them outside Leinster House.

●●●●●★●●●●●

Careers you'd think would be a credit, but aren't:

★ Nurse. Too sexy.

★ Garda: police are just too prone to breaking up fun evenings. Female guards used to be called *Bean Gardaí* (pronounced "ban") so you'd know even without looking at them that this wasn't a man-guard you were dealing with. But then it was discovered that both sexes went up against bad guys unarmed in exactly the same way, and both were equally fond of raiding lock-ins if they weren't on the guest list, and they were granted equal billing.

★ Nun. Just that bit *too* sweet to be wholesome. Anyone hiding their bold streak this well must really be very bold altogether.

★ IT or tech whizz. Too brainy so probably not to be trusted. Ahead of the curve. Don't know their place.

★ Farmer. A woman can't be a farmer, silly. She can be a farmer's wife, though, which means running the farm, calving the cows and doing all the same farm work the fellas do, while also making the dhinner. Over-achiever.

TARA FLYNN

How To Give Terrible Customer Service

·····

Welcoming we may be, but we all know that customer service in Ireland doesn't even come close to Grand. Tourists get the good stuff, the air hostess stuff, and we get what's left over, which really isn't very good at all. But you see, if we went the extra mile for a customer we'd probably have to overstep some mark or other, and that might involve having to leave our place.

Just in case you've been well trained in customer service in your own career, and would like to learn how it's done here, here you go:

★ Say "I don't know". Often. Before you've even heard the end of the query. This works equally well on the phone as in person.

★ Make sure you do not volunteer anything: information, a refund, an offer to find an answer to what it is that you don't know. Nothing.

★ Your superior is out. Where? You don't know. Act like you've never heard of the concept of a superior before. Eventually, say, "Oh, that's me."

★ Wear a blank expression, and when it feels like you've said "I don't know" so often that the customer is thinking about murdering you, shrug. Just the once, though. Shrugs are for flavour. Don't take the piss.

★ If a customer is returning something, say a meal or a jumper, stare at the returned item in silence for several minutes. Do not move. Let the customer wait while you come up with your surprise reaction …

★ … which is to suddenly stop being still and go off into the kitchen or phone head office and tut and roll your eyes about the customer.

★ By this stage, the jumper should have fully unravelled or the meal be completely cold. The customer should be full-on murderous by now, and you'd be wise to remove any cutlery or knitting needles from their vicinity.

★ Eventually, the customer – unless they're a robot – will get very angry and say things like "This isn't good enough. I paid good money. I'm never doing business with you again." Try not to smile, which will be difficult because this is what you've been aiming for all along – to get them out of your bored, bored face. In

a joyless monotone, say, "There's no need to shout at me, sir."

★ Have 999 on speed dial because he may have a heart attack by this point.

★ Once the ambulance door shuts, Congratulations! You have given customer service at an Irish level. The next level up is American Teen – but I don't think you're ready for that yet.

Fancy Goods: Advertising and Marketing

• • • • •

Advertising in Ireland was traditionally all aimed at women. We were the ones going to the shops, the only acceptable place to be outside the home for a woman who knows her place. There would be maybe two ads on TV for men each day, at teatime, when it was presumed they were in being served The Tay. Ads about brucellosis or mastitis in cattle – oh yes, because the men would obviously be farmers, grabbing a bite before heading back out to do manly work, leaving the wife to do the washing up – after she'd brought in the cows, calving a couple en route, of course.

Before we had TV, ads basically took the form of the tin sign outside a shop selling "Fancy Goods". That was all you needed

to know, because you already knew what was in the other shops and whether you needed any of it. Then, ads evolved, targeting Irish women like this:

★ *"Hurry, hurry, hurry …"* There might be a crowd in the way, you've a lot on, but you won't want to miss this. I'll say it 3 times, in case you missed the first one.

★ *"That's right!"* It was obviously decided that Irish women were either a bit deaf or a biteen slow and that you'd responded to the TV or wireless aloud. It's probably why we have so many reports of hauntings and apparitions. It was just ads, answering us back.

★ *"Ladies …"* Most ads started this way. Superfluous, because we were the only ones watching unless it was *The Late Late Show* or a match, but it showed that they knew what we liked. And we love to be called ladies. I'm getting my dainty purse out right now, just thinking about it.

★ *"Don't Forget …"* Market research obviously showed that we were a dizzy bunch.

★ *"Have a pint …"* These are new. Shocking when they came out. But women can order pints in ads with abandon now, reflecting the

fact that it's happening in the real world too.

We've come a long way since all they wanted us to buy was shortening, perfume and Bovril. Oh, and public service announcements featuring tractors and how not to die in fires. But have you ever run out of shortening, perfume or Bovril? Of course you haven't. Advertising works.

It might be time to have a closer look at the media in Ireland, just for a laugh.

How To Get on Television

In Ireland, getting on television used to be relatively easy. Now it's so easy you don't even have to think about it. Everyone's on TV! It's one of our favourite pastimes. You're probably on right now – have you checked?

Once we discovered reality shows, we were away on a hack. (Actually, someone is surely pitching "Away on a Hack": something involving horses and the internet, ideal for a Sunday evening now that *Little House on the Prairie* is only on TG4 during the week these days.)

Time was you had to be a politician, a Eurovision hopeful, a cool priest or someone who actually worked at the station to get on TV. Now, from the minute they've had their first appearance as an annoying toddler on *The Late Late Toy Show* at Christmas, Irish people are never off TV. The population is so small, they

eventually get around to broadcasting everyone.

But if you haven't been on yet don't worry. You're Grand. The best course of action is:

•••••★•••••

Agree on stuff.

Sing (harp optional but strongly advised).

Be religious.

Be good at Irish dancing.

Be religious about Irish dancing.

Have a puppet.

Be good at Make & Do. Holding scissors "like a bunch of flowers", that sort of thing.

Have really, really long eyelashes, As if a giant exotic moth landed on your face and you might just take flight in a stiff wind.

Hold an extreme position. For "balance".

Become a sexy meteorologist. NOT TOO SEXY – we're not able.

Make homemade jam or jumpers "down the country".

Be awesome like Miriam O'Callaghan.

•••••★•••••

VIP:
Very Irish Person
(CELEBRITY)
•••••

Here's how we treat famous people in Ireland: we leave them alone. Some are grateful for it, some feel ignored.

The truth is, we don't want to give anyone the soot of realising we knew who they were. In fact, the way you recognise a truly famous person in Ireland is that they're the one everyone's looking away from.

> **MADE UP FACT #3** Bono can't get served in the centre of Dublin.

You want to be the best Irishwoman you can be. I get it. But be careful in case you get too well known for it, because next comes the inevitable begrudgery. It's "You think you're great" supersized. You simply can't be Grand and have a big head, or you'll have all that pride knocked out of you.

Conversely if you show you don't have a big head, and go into town for a pint like a normal person, everyone will descend on you to show their appreciation. We never said we weren't contrary (in fact, we've said little else). But hopefully you're finding that delightful.

YOU'RE GRAND

4

Ireland is so small that everyone already knows you. Once you get a bit famous – whether you're on TV, radio, in the papers or made a viral cat video – especially OUTSIDE IRELAND – you will be feted in story and song. But if you're a bighead about it, the songs will be really short and have a lot of swear words in them.

As we've seen in "How to Get on Television", at some point, you will probably be a celebrity in Ireland. It's hard to avoid. So here are some dos and don'ts for being a famous Irishwoman and staying Grand:

DO

★ Engage a stylist immediately. Jumpers just don't look great on the covers of magazines. At the very least you'll need to accessorise and you should not attempt this by yourself.

★ You must make appearances at a really horrible late-night bar where they don't even serve pints and nobody's ever met your da. It should have a name like *Gloss* or *Klubb* or *Spew*.

★ Do at-home photoshoots in someone else's house. Not because you're ashamed of your own, but because you wouldn't give the general public the soot of seeing where you really live.

★ Get to know all the other celebs. You already do, from home, so this is easy.

★ Release a single. You only need to sell about 10 copies to get to the top of the Irish charts so congratulations in advance! If you don't break the Top 20, are you sure you told your family the single was out?

DON'T

★ Forget your high heels. But because these are foreign to us, just stand in one spot, posing.

★ Discuss your politics or real opinions. Ever. It doesn't matter if it's true, it may very well get you sued.

★ Date another celebrity. Feeling like they know both of you will just wreck people's heads.

★ Turn down a job. Even if it's an ad for something terrible like a puppy cannon and you strongly don't believe in puppy cannons, you must appear in the ad, stuffing puppies down the pipe. Otherwise, word will get out that you think you're great and too good for the job. Loads of other people would jump at the chance to be a puppy cannon-stuffer. People in the industry talk.

★ Talk about anyone. As with the previous point, the country is TOO SMALL to bring up anyone specific, even in a positive light. By the

time Irish whispers do their thing, everyone
will believe that you said that thing about your
colleague not even being capable of loading a
puppy cannon.

You can be famous in Ireland for many more things than being
on *The Voice*, which seems to be how all the other countries are
doing it now. Here are a few options for women:

●●●●● ★ ●●●●●

Getting an A in Home Economics
Being a Young Scientist of the Year (good
  girl yourself)
Being President
Writing about other women and their exploits
  or sexploits
Winning the Eurovision
Being super-holy
Defying someone super-holy
Having even a walk-on part in a film or TV
  show OUTSIDE IRELAND
Riding horses really well
Knowing loads of rhymes
Sporty punching
Going into space (this hasn't happened yet,

but imagine)
Having a giant, magic cloak (this has)

●●●●● ★ ●●●●●

Fame is always a double-edged sword, nowhere more so than in Ireland. It's easy, but it's hard. And you'll have to work really hard to find out who your real friends are. So, just like normal Irish people, so.

Women Aren't Funny

●●●●●

Only men are funny. Women aren't funny. Because women who are funny don't know their place. Even Irish women (who we all know are hilarious)? Not funny. I don't care if you've written ten jokes or have just made the postman laugh, (a) there's no way those jokes can be funny and (b) you still know your postman? That must be a nice place you have there.

> **MADE UP FACT #4** You probably thought that laughter came from the brain, from what made up experts call the "Humour Centre". WRONG. Funny doesn't come from there. It comes from the penis. All laughter springs fully formed from the penis of a man for the hilarity and enjoyment of other humans.

It's useless to try to fight the preconception that women aren't funny, or point out that it's insulting and inaccurate. And massively sexist. But so many journalists continue to bring it up that it seems we've been wrong: it is *very* relevant. It is current and pressing. The "unfunny women chestnut", instead of being dull, unimaginative, lazy journalism, is in fact the vital probing of an ancient mystery. The bottom line being that women should stay home, knowing their place and laughing at what comes out of their partner's penis.

Cappuccino, Yes

• • • • •

For most women in Ireland, peace, contentment and generally being Grand came from not having to make any pesky decisions: one channel on the telly, one true religion, one-screen cinemas and no such thing as pizza. It might sound shite but it was very freeing. It was easy to know your place, and having no other options meant we had a lot of spare time to write poems.

Coffee came out of a jar and was white or black. But then, around the year 2000, everything changed. We got a Cappuccino Culture. The country leapt to the sound of milk frothing and coffee menus being nailed to walls. A menu ... *for coffee? Even down the country.* Our heads exploded in a mess of latte froth.

From there, it was a slippery slope to losing the run of ourselves and sliding out of our place, and gaining some brand

new stereotypes along with it. Now that we had more, we wanted even more. Chocolate bars were fancier. Frizzy hair could be straightened. THE INTERNET. Consternation was widespread. Shops sprang up selling just cheese. A shop for just cheese. Hundreds of different kinds. Until recently there were just 3: lunch cheese, posh cheese and plastic I'm-making-a-cheeseburger-that-could-outlast-a-nuclear-winter cheese. That was it. Now, we didn't know where to look.

To begin with, all that plenty was enjoyable. But this is Ireland: it was never going to last.

'Tis Far from Brunches We Were Reared: A New Steroetype
·····

During these times, which became known as the "Celtic Tiger", Irish women tried a new stereotype out for size. We look back on it now and shudder. In a nutshell, we got monopoly money from a fake property boom, there were teeth-whitening places on every corner, our heads were fried from too many kinds of cheese, and teenagers thought it was OK to buy €4,000 handbags. The poor kids. Where were their iMOMs, with their Irishwomanly certainty that misery must be only just around the corner? Because it was. In 2008, the entire country was left by a moneyed few in negative equity, jobless and despondent.

The €4,000 handbags had to be sold for half that on eBay, to pay for flights to Australia. We had nothing but re-runs of *Sex and the City* to remind us of the brunches that we used to have.

During the Celtic Tiger, brunch was practically all we ate. Deafened by hollandaise and blinded by the aforementioned cappuccino froth, we lost sight of The Breakfast, The Dhinner and The Tay, along with the run of ourselves.

The new stereotype didn't fit us terribly well at all. Greedy, materialistic and loads of other things that you mightn't ordinarily associate with Ireland, and most definitely not with Irish women. We should really be grateful for the austerity measures that brought us crashing back to some Grand sense.

••••• ★ •••••

CHARACTERISTICS OF THE CELTIC TIGRESS

★ We focussed more on our looks than ever before. We were white-toothed, orange, smooth-haired *crathers* – a little bit like tigers ourselves.

★ We got loads of cosmetic surgery. Irish women! We went from not caring what people thought to trying to look exactly like other people, all with the exact same frozen face.

★ Probably just as well, then, that it was hard to catch sight of us, driving around too fast in our brand new cars. You'd have at least one, but probably more. Spare cars would be used for storage, or as ashtrays at a barbecue, or to keep your spare car keys in. No one would bother stealing them – they had plenty cars of their own.

★ Irish women aren't built to compete against each other, and certainly not for stuff. Stuff's not important to us: it's too easily lost in a fire or a flood or to the English. We forgot that for a minute there.

Truth is, Irish women never function better than when we're in crisis. So, post-crash, here we are more tiger than ever, teeth and claws bared and ready for action. We may have a few more stress lines now, but guess what? We couldn't give a feck. 'Twas far from brunches we were reared. We remember our place now. We won't leave it again.

While we're talking about new stereotypes, there is another less prevalent but still important one that merits a mention.

Supermammy, Stepford Mammy

•••••

Another facet of the newly emerging Ireland is that it's abandoning religion at a rate faster than almost any other country. We're just reporting it, so don't blame us, St Patrick! Sadly, after thousands of years of their "go" not being enough for them, some extreme religious folk are appalled at the rise of a more secular society in Ireland. Loudly, and all the time. We seem to be witnessing the arrival of a brand new Irish female archetype. A kind of Stepford iMOM who reckons she can have it all: career, kids and time to be on every TV show ever, being appalled.

If this archetype's mind weren't so closed, she might be a pretty awesome role model. She knows not just her own place, but all of our places and she'll put you back in yours with just a steely gaze. But her mind is as shut as the pleats on her calf-length skirt are straight. Only cis-gendered, God-fearing, male/female couples are allowed, and if you don't want children … well, she'll smile at you but she thinks you're a freak. But she'll say it so sweetly! With no swearing! And she wears pearls! She's just lovely, really.

These women present a reasonable face, but look out: inequality is their thing, and Ireland's moving on without them. They're welcome to their beliefs, pleats and all, but in all honesty, telling anyone else that they shouldn't have the kind of craic they want is just a bit too unIrish for the rest of our liking.

Grand Finance

•••••

We've seen the short-lived Celtic Tigress, and how greed led us to fall flat on our uncharacteristically botoxed faces. So how should an Irishwoman deal with money?

The great thing is that if you're a proper traditional Irishwoman, your husband will be taking care of all of that. Besides, you won't have any leftovers after feeding and clothing your several childer. But if you have nothing to spend on but your own selfish independent whims, then you might have to be more careful.

The problem is that Irish women just can't do the "short-term pain for long-term gain" thing. We know there'll be long-term pain either way, so we want to have our fun now and then enjoy the worry and guilt forever. So we have split financial personalities:

WHAT WE SHOULD SPEND MONEY ON	WHAT WE ACTUALLY SPEND IT ON
Taxes	Sun holidays. These will make us more productive, therefore more useful in the workforces, therefore better able to pay taxes – next year
Health insurance	Sun holidays
Staycations & supporting local tourism	Sun holidays
Public transport	Cars we can't afford to put petrol in
Umbrellas	Sunglasses. For sun holidays

WHERE WE SHOULD PUT OUR SAVINGS	WHERE WE ACTUALLY PUT OUR SAVINGS
Under the mattress, in a hole in a field, anywhere but a bank	What savings?

100,000 Welcomes

• • • • •

And so we come full circle to the only bit of income we can really trust: tourism. Not even the rain puts those guys off!

Every '70s postcard – all cartoon colours, red-headed donkeys and turf – makes Ireland seem very inviting. And it is. Not for the people who have to emigrate to get jobs, and not for people being evicted all over again (this time by banks instead of landlords), but still. Aren't we grand and don't we have the craic?

We want everyone from overseas to know that we'll be rolling out the green carpet as soon as they are deposited here by the iMOMs of the Sky. You'll have heard it first from them in their sounds-like-Irish: *Céad Míle Fáilte* – One Hundred Thousand Welcomes. I'm sure you'll agree, that's an awful lot of welcomes. Imagine having to generate them? It's a lot of pressure, but it's worth it.

Any Irish women growing up in the '70s and '80s learned fairly quickly that without tourism, there would be no jobs in Ireland AT ALL. We'd all have to emigrate and then we'd be the tourists and who'd be here to welcome us, AT ALL AT ALL?

So we had to be prepared to make all of them feel welcome. *Irish* welcome. That's more welcome than most people can comfortably handle.

I'm not going to give you 100,000 tips on how to do an Irish Welcome, or as it could be known "sucking up to foreigners". I'm sure you can come up with your own. But here are the basics to start you off:

★ Smile. Even if your face hurts, even if they try to make fun of your teeth. Irish people have great teeth now and great cosmetic dentistry. Smile from the minute they walk up your path til the minute you shut the door behind them. Don't worry if it seems fake. The last thing a welcome needs is sincerity. Authenticity: yes. Sincerity: nah.

MADE UP FACT #5 The Tourist Board was behind the teeth-whitening boom. Whiter smiles are like beacons to tourists.

COTTAGE INDUSTRY ALERT: Cosmetic dentistry home visits. All you need is some porcelain, a van, and one of those gurgly things dentists have.

★ Speak some Irish. You can make a lot of it up, like Ronald Reagan did when he came and said … *something* … but nobody knew what it was. They all clapped anyway. Give the *cúpla focail* a go so people will know you're the real deal.

★ Bow a bit when passing a tourist, or at least

incline your head. Even if you don't have a cap to doff, deference is what's expected of us.

★ Be hilarious. Easy. This will usually happen when you use your mouth to speak as people copy our accent or repeat back to us phrases with which they're unfamiliar because they don't travel or read. You didn't know you were hilarious (especially seeing as women aren't funny), but because of your accent, you are!

★ Feed them. Keep feeding. Set a table with ham salad, soup, a full dhinner and 20 cakes OR just throw it all in a cement mixer and let them chow down in a trough. That way you can keep it coming without having to worry about dishes. Besides, they probably only eat smoothies where they come from, anyway.

MADE UP FACT #6 Most tourists have forgotten how to chew.

★ Sing.

★ Make shit up. Give them the wrong directions. Tell them the fridge is haunted. Bit mean, but it'll keep you sane and maybe even buy you a few minutes to yourself while they check the Smeg for ghosts.

★ Lie. *Yes, you did make that brown bread. The plastic brown bread package in the bin is a leprechaun raincoat. Yes! They do exist!*

★ Light a big roaring fire. Tricky if you don't have a fireplace, but you're an Irishwoman – you'll think of something. Throw a match to the couch. If you don't have a fire, what the feck are you going to tell stories by?

★ Pretend not to have electricity and that you have to walk 3 miles for water from the nearest spring or pump. People are so much more grateful for that hot dhinner or lukewarm shower when they believe you've gone through immense hardship to make them happen.

★ Dance. Preferably at a crossroads.

★ Give good customer service. But ONLY to US visitors. Everyone else finds our ineptitude charming, but Americans will not put up with that shit.

★ Wear a giant Aran jumper. It will be the biggest financial outlay in your Welcome-To-Ireland pack but it will be worth it. It'll keep you warm, it'll prove your Irishness, it will mean you don't even have to think about what to wear every day, like poor Beyoncé.

TARA FLYNN

• • • • • ★ • • • • •

What should be in your Welcome-To-Ireland pack: matches, a song book, an English-Irish dictionary, a tweed cap, tea bags, an Aran jumper, The Dress (more on which later), a laying hen, a local bus timetable and a harp. You're welcome.

• • • • • ★ • • • • •

An Irishwoman Abroad

• • • • •

Irish women have always gone abroad, whether we liked it or not. Mostly, we didn't like it. With enforced travel like coffin ships to America, deportation to Australia for FREE if you stole a loaf of bread, or the entire female population of Baltimore, Co. Cork, being abducted by pirates in 1631, we soon got a taste for it. With all the scurvy and death, we felt right at home.

It's only in the last couple of decades that Irish women have had the money or the wherewithal to travel *and come back*. In the past, you either went somewhere never to return, or you stayed put. No Graaaahnd Victorian tours for us. But we're making up for lost travel time now, with a vengeance.

Irish men abroad have always liked to leave their mark – with railroads and such – and Irish women are no different.

144

Here are some of the ways you can spot an Irishwoman off her home turf:

★ If she doesn't already have "a lovely colour" she'll be working her way up to it. She'll be on the beach by 9am, having been to the market at dawn to buy olive oil and lemon juice with which to baste herself.

★ She will have sussed where the nearest Irish bar is as soon as she lands, especially if they stream GAA games.

★ She will drop into the Irish consulate on day two, because she feels a bit homesick. Relatively, the more she referred to Ireland as "this kip" before she left, the sooner the consulate will hear from her. Generally, as the plane departs from an Irish airport, she realises her mistake.

★ Irish women abroad suddenly get very picky. They send food back, say "I miss my mammy's dhinner" and head straight back to the Irish bar, starving, hoping against hope they sell Tayto crisps or at least have some gravy.

★ Speaking of which, Irish women abroad are the ones arriving with suitcases bulging with Tayto, tea bags and butter or meat that it's

probably illegal to transport, but they're willing to take the risk.

★ Irish women are as friendly abroad as they are at home, and mix well with the locals. From Barcelona to Beijing, the ultimate compliment is "You're just like us!"

Despite our protestations, once an Irish person leaves Ireland, it's as if a limb has been cut off. We take it for granted til it's not there. Then we cry and write poems about how amazing it is. Until the returning plane lands. As the nice tourists clap the pilot and "ooh" about how green the runway is, you'll hear the natives quietly whisper one word: "Kip."

Irish Roots Denial

• • • • •

There is a terrible kind of Irishwoman that we didn't think you'd be ready to meet until now. The Irish Roots Denier. Too awful to contemplate. She knows her place alright, it's just that she'd rather forget it.

This is an Irishwoman who wakes up every day, wishing she weren't Irish. She spends years trying to disguise any association with us. "I'm not Irish, really I'm not." Note the "really" in the wrong place, so you might even think she were English.

The term West Brit is a derogatory one, used to sum up this kind of person. But it's a bit too harsh. Firstly, as already discussed, there's nothing wrong with being a "Brit" and we've loads to thank them for. Secondly, the term is a kind of disowning, when our goal should be to welcome these stray sheep back to the fold. We must put away the fingers of judgement and hold out the jumpers of welcome.

Irish Roots Deniers in the US and Australia are descendants who have washed their hands of St Patrick and wouldn't go near green if you paid them. They won't even step on grass for fear of becoming one with it. That's a lot of missed picnics and that's very sad.

If you know someone like this – someone who insists on saying "Boxing Day" when they obviously mean "Stephen'ses Day", or mangles words like *Nuacht* (News) on purpose for fear they'll be asked to speak Irish – give them a wide berth. Ready the jumpers of welcome, but it's only by first feeling the cold that these lambs will crave our acceptance and wool. They are one of us, but there's no point trying to convince them. Besides, the realisation will mean so much more having come to it themselves. But you can bet on this: no matter what they say during their lifetime, there's not one of them who won't have 'Danny Boy' sung at her funeral.

GTA:
Grand Tough Auto
····

While we're here talking travel, how do Irish women who stay put get around? It's true, we are great walkers. But sometimes, you just need to get somewhere faster, and without the head being blown off you by the wind and rain. For that, you need a grand, solid car. But is it possible to know your place if you're driving away from it?

In years gone by you would only see Irish women driving in real life. Never in ads. In films, posh Irish women were driven while poor ones walked in mud, all the way to America. You might see a screen Irishwoman driving if a man had some kind of medical emergency or had died and left her the use of the car. In postcards, Irish women usually drove cattle, ahead of them, along with some hilarious joke about traffic in Ireland. Haha hahaha haha ha.

MADE UP FACT #7 Irish women are the best drivers in Europe. The most courteous anyway, and the cause of way fewer accidents. Why? We wouldn't give men the soot of making shite jokes about Lady Drivers. They would try, but we would come after them …

} driving really slowly, with the lights off, down
a deserted country lane. }

In real life, women drove lots and drove well. They drove
because public transport was terrible and they had stuff they
wanted to get done. Oh, Londoners had it so easy with their
regular buses and Tubes! We didn't have those, so we got a lot of
practice behind the wheel. We even had a famous woman rally
driver called Rosemary Smith! No one could say she wasn't a
good driver. It was very exciting.

During the Celtic Tiger times you'd practically change
your car every night, like underwear. The discomfort caused by
having "last year's" registration plate drove many to … well …
drive to a dealership to get the most up to date model available.
It was silly. But we love cars almost as much as we love horses in
this country, so much so that we refuse to eat either.

Until relatively recently, it was possible to drive on a provisional
licence forever in Ireland, so nobody had to take a test. It was like
an assault course out there. No wonder we're so good.

If you've never seen the majesty of an Irishwoman atop a Massey
Ferguson tractor, towering above all she surveys, in full command
and fully aware of her power, you have not known true might.

● ● ● ● ● ★ ● ● ● ● ●

OTHER GRAND MODES OF TRANSPORT

Hitchhiking: Don't hitchhike in Ireland. Aside from the usual, obvious dangers, in Ireland there's an even greater peril: the chatty driver. Someone who lives alone, or as good as alone with someone they've long since stopped talking to. Someone who'll take you twice the distance you wanted to go in case you'd miss out on a single detail of their life story. Someone so cut off from the rest of the planet that they're still picking up hitchhikers. At some point, you'll probably have the urge to fling yourself out at highspeed, tucking and rolling your way to freedom, without so much as a backward glance at your backpack.

Taxis: Similar to the hitchhiking scenario in terms of chattiness. Pray you don't get a friendly driver. He will tell you terrible jokes and it's all very awkward. Only marginally better is a grumpy one, who will still be chatty, but at least he won't wait for a response. It requires a lot less energy. A grumpy taxi driver will mainly say things like "This shower" or "Pile of gobballoons" in some kind of unflattering

reference to the government. (That's if he doesn't actually call them much, much worse.)

Buses: Probably the best way for an Irishwoman to get around since donkeys went out. It's social, but there's room to get away from chatters if you want to. If you're up for the chat yourself, there's loads of craic to be had. The Irish women who make the best use of the bus are the little old ladies with the free travel. They put on the good dress and the good coat and meet their friends down the back of the bus and go on an outing. They solve all the problems of the world with a lot of tutting. And a lot of laughing. The ladies on the bus would almost make you wish you were old enough for the free travel. Almost.

•••••★•••••

Nobody's Heard of Us

•••••

Growing up as a woman in Ireland, you get told over and over that – although you yourself personally are probably a bit useless – Irish men were heroes, poets, saints, scholars and probably rides as well. You didn't hear a lot about Irish women

doing cool stuff, but feck it, the lads sounded great. We took the reflected glory of their renown and were glad of it. It was great to feel that such a small country had such an important place in the world.

So we get an awful shock when we step outside Ireland for the first time and realise that nobody's actually heard of us at all. They don't know where Ireland is, or they think it's in Britain, or they think it only appears once every hundred years, out of the mist, like Brigadoon. Maybe that's why our trains are so erratic – they can't be sure if the next station actually exists.

While we assume that Arthur Guinness, Oscar Wilde, Joyce, Yeats and saints Patrick, Brendan and Bono are being discussed over breakfast all over the world, there are American teens who've never heard of us at all. They think Jay-Z put us on the map in 2014 just by coming here and walking around, which was very nice of Jay-Z. French people think you're mispronouncing "Iceland" or "Holland" because they've never heard of Irlande … and half of them have been here for the rugby.

That's just the countries with which we have special relationships (i.e. who we suck up to the most for the tourist euros). Nobody else even knows we exist.

Because you don't think you're great, even you might buckle and begin to agree that maybe Ireland doesn't exist. The Strypes might even be on the radio at the time but you pretend not to hear them, just so's not to contradict someone who's not

Irish, because they must know stuff. But hold firm. Ireland does exist. Here are a few ways you can prove it:

• • • • • ★ • • • • •

Proof that Ireland exists:

The Pope didn't disappear in 1979. He has to have gone somewhere.

Ulysses: you couldn't make it up. Even Joyce had his limits.

There'd have been no transatlantic travel without somewhere to refuel. We're the original pit stop .

Rain has to have somewhere to land, other than plains in Spain.

All those films made here.

That awful "Oirish" accent people do has to be based on something.

Riverdance.

I know that's not a lot of proof, but it is scientific. It'll do. It's Grand.

• • • • • ★ • • • • •

Nobody Expects the Irish Inquisition

•••••

The only thing an Irishwoman likes better than knowing her own place is knowing everyone else's. You could say "we have a childlike curiosity about all things and people." Or you could tell the truth: we're nosy.

No one is as nosy as an Irishwoman. There's a certain honesty to the way Irish women look for information; they won't really try to pretend they're doing anything else. So, to be more like an Irishwoman, ask more questions. You're a kind of modern-day Columbo, seeking out even the most seemingly insignificant of clues:

Which way was he facing when he said that?

Had he a bag with him?

Did she make that phonecall before or after lunch?

Would you say there was a light wind blowing, or more of a stiff breeze?

Had they drink taken?

Who are you and what do you want?

What's this button for? Should I press it? Oh, should I not press it?

What should I do if I'm just after pressing it?

The kind of interrogation an Irish parent (an iMOM in particular) can deliver is lethal. If they can extract the most sensitive of info from a total stranger, imagine how effective they are with someone about whom they have prior knowledge.

•••••★•••••

Curtains

•••••

Curtains keep a grand bit of heat in, and the summer sun off the telly when the Angelus is on, it's true.
But the real reason an Irishwoman chooses curtains is spying.

MADE UP FACT #8 Net curtains are considered highly dangerous by the CIA.
A CIA fella would have better luck tracking down the Taliban than getting up
Mrs. O'Shea's garden path unobserved.

Blinds make a noise when you part them, and the tell-tale vertical crack is an instant giveaway to an outside observer. Useless. You even have to put your fingers through to get

a proper look. There's a subtlety to curtains that means you can even be having a look at what's going on outside from a few feet back, while enjoying a grand cup of tea. Every Irishwoman knows that knowledge is power, and knowledge acquired in the presence of tea is unbeatable.

This isn't about being sneaky, but a bit of gossip about the eejit election campaigner with the toupee that blew off in your garden never hurt anybody.

You don't need a lie detector; you just need an Irishwoman. We have a nose for bullshit like nobody else. We've smelled enough of it.

Hopefully this has shown that one of the most important keys to being Grand is knowing your place. Keep just enough of a rein on that undeniable bold streak, and you won't go too far astray.

5

GRAND HOBBIES AND PASTIMES

★

When she's not being in iMOM, what does an Irishwoman get up to? Is it possible to leave the house and still be Grand? There's a lot to tempt you off the Grand path out there, it's true. But we're here to make sure you never stray too far.

The Hangover: Part You

Irish women may have a reputation for wildness, but we're actually pretty shy. (That'll be the years of hearing that our innate boldness should be squished back into its place.) Left to our own devices, many of us wouldn't leave the house, just as traditional Ireland would like it. With nature pulling us one way and tradition another, it can be very confusing. But sooner or later we say "feck that" and head to the pub.

Alcohol is a serious drug, and alcoholism is a terrible

problem in Ireland for men and women alike. The Drunken Irish stereotype still hangs over every bar stool. But that's not to say you can't enjoy a drink or our wonderful pub culture "responsibly", like the ads say.

Why do we "drown our sorrows" so much here? Well, honestly, we've had a lot of sorrows to drown: the Essions alone would wear you out. We've learned to be suspicious and reserved: alcohol relaxes us and loosens our tongues back to our more natural state. And let's not let the weather off the hook: if Ireland were sunnier, maybe we wouldn't look so forward to a warming whiskey by the fire. If we had better summers, maybe wine wouldn't seem so delicious: sometimes the switch from red to white is the only mark of the change in seasons, from "wet" to "slightly-warmer-but-still-wet".

We all know alcohol doesn't solve anything and is no substitute for professional help if things are bad. But a few glasses to mark a celebration, or wet a baby's head, or commiserate when Ireland loses (again) are part of who we are.

There's a perception in Ireland that drinking adds to "the craic". If no craic is being had, there's a belief that a pint will create some. If craic is already in progress, imagine how much more craic they could be having if they had a pint.

Then, there's the unparalleled peer pressure. It's not that we're mad for drink, it's that we're bad at saying "No". "Go on, you will. You will of course. Juice? Are you sick? Sure, a drink

will make you feel better." We are also just so feckin' persuasive.

Basically, if you want to avoid tomorrow's hangover, a ton of empty calories and another "situation" with Jim from accounts, you'd do well to have a strategy in place in advance.

•••••★•••••

HOW NOT TO DRINK

★ Say you have an evening of operating heavy machinery planned.

★ Order soft drinks in shot glasses.

★ Pretend there's already vodka in your Coke.

★ The last two mean you'll have to get every round in or have your cover blown. Bring a roll of cash.

★ Say you're on antibiotics. Act sick for about a week in the run-up, to make it "stick".

★ Drink a pint and streeeeetch it.

★ Change your religion to one of the non-drinky ones.

★ Stand firm and breathe: in a couple of pints' time, no one else will notice what you're drinking.

★ Fake the world's longest pregnancy.

•••••★•••••

Hangover: If you live in Ireland, chances are that at some stage even these rock-solid strategies will fail, and you'll wake up dying from a hangover. Even if it's an epic one, you probably won't end up in Vegas with a tiger; it's more likely to be Dr Quirkey's Good Time Emporium with a stray cat. And which of us hasn't been there?

There are a few ways to cope.

THE MORNING AFTER:

★ Fuzzy on the details? Don't worry. Despite having drunk as much as you, your drinking companions will remember every single nuance, and be happy to recount each one for you on a crowded bus or in the middle of a presentation. The more embarrassing, the better. It's funny because it didn't happen to them.

★ Eat a full Irish breakfast. Extra grease. Extra salt.

★ Drink red lemonade. (It's a real thing. No, we don't know what red lemons are, either.)

★ Wear your pain like a badge of honour. Be ultra dramatic about it.

★ Use descriptive words in close proximity to

fully convey how awful you feel: hangin', dying, self-inflicted, and grown woman. Say the phrase "Never again" at least 20 times an hour.

★ Google reviews of the new pub down the road. Arrange to meet everyone there for the hair of the dog. But this time, you'll have chips before instead of after. You know, for soakage.

SOAKAGE

Soakage is what you eat before you drink to "soak" up the alcohol. It is considered a highly mature and responsible action. Scientific, even. Maybe just drink less ...? Oh, well, anyway:

★ Good sources of soakage: toast, peanuts, chips, anything from Abrakebabra, pints of milk, raw eggs (champion drinkers only – they have no stomach lining left, obviously).

★ Refer to whatever you're eating as "soakage" aloud, so everyone knows how wise you are. e.g. "Give us a packet of those bacon fries, please, barman. Soakage." And wink. He will nod back, acknowledging your wisdom.

DRINKING AND DRIVING
Don't
•••••★•••••

Ireland would be a very different place if we weren't drinkers. Uncomfortable with sober touching since de-paganising, we might have died out long ago. Or even more people would have emigrated because they'd all have woken up on time and made their flights. The country would just be a big, green rock, floating in the Atlantic, weighted down only by hundreds of thousands of empty bottles, pint glasses and kegs.

A Pint of Plain Is Your Only (Wo) Man
•••••

Speaking of alcohol, is pub culture Grand for Irish women?

These days we take for granted that Irish women love a pint. Surely we always have, haven't we? NO. It's only in the last couple of decades that Irish women have been allowed to have pints at all. Read that again: <u>we were not allowed pints.</u> Maybe they thought the glasses were too big for our tiny hands? If a woman got served a pint, say if she was in a particularly convincing disguise, she had to have it in two separate glasses.

It made for an awful lot of washing up.

The cute little "snugs" in pubs that tourists and overly amorous couples like so much nowadays were the place for the women to hang out. Not by choice: to keep them apart from the men. Sure all kinds of shenanigans could happen if men and women drank in the same room (ironically, the sort of shenanigans now taking place between amorous couples in pubs in snugs). Women would be handed drinks occasionally through a little hatch. Kind of like a confessional, with drink.

Mná Mná: The Long Walk to the Jacks

•••••

The great thing about Irish pubs is that women can't get too drunk because there's a built-in safeguard. There being no women in pubs back in the day, there were no provisions made for women's toilets. So now, when nature calls, you have to trek all the way to the back of the building, down a corridor, out a door, along an enchanted smoking passage*, passing sherpas, explorers and yetis on your way: rest assured, the Ladies' will be MILES AWAY. It will have been added about 500 years after the rest of the pub, and it will be freezing. The Irish answer to an age-old mystery is easy: why do women go to the loo in

pairs? FOR WARMTH. By the time you get back to your seat, you will be completely sober and a little bit fitter. Who says pubs are bad for your health?

When you eventually get there, you will of course recognise the Ladies' in an Irish pub by the word "Mná". The rule is you have to say it twice, like the Muppet song. It livens up even the dreariest Friday evening/is really super annoying, depending on your mood.

Loos in Irish pubs are referred to as "the jacks". Never "jills". That's more of it now.

•••••★•••••

THE SMOKING BAN

The pub has always been a great place to take refuge, out of the vile, dank weather and into a vile, dank atmosphere of welcome. The walls and ceilings, yellow from cigarette smoke, were like sun to us. Then in 2004, they took the sun away.

Ireland was the first country in the world to ban smoking in workplaces – pubs included – and people nearly died from the shock. "We banned *what*? From *where*?"

Sure, it was a great idea health-wise, but no one thought it would catch on. "Now we'll be

able to see everyone clearly!" we moaned. Little old men, their lungs emptying of toxins by the minute, died of nostalgia instead.

And then, someone invented the beer garden. They didn't exist pre-2004, because the whole point of pubs was getting inside. But now, anything could be a beer garden:

★ the back passage en route to the Mná
★ the "porch" (a garden umbrella in a barrel)
★ some bars just stuck a table and chairs up the chimney. No one ever complained.

As smoking is now a rogue act, you'll often find single Irish women outside, pretending to smoke, eyes (and noses and lungs) peeled for fellow rogues.

• • • • • ★ • • • • •

How To Look Grand "In This Weather"

• • • • •

The truth is that Irish weather is another one of those clichés we wish weren't true, but are. You really don't know what to expect from one minute to the next, let alone what you should wear all

the way into the evening if you're planning it earlier that day. Even if you look out your window and make a dash for the door, by the time you've turned your key in the lock, you could still be wrong. Clouds spill out of nowhere into enormous puddles, hot spells melt you into puddles; basically, there are puddles no matter what the sky is up to. Suede is never an option.

So how do you stay looking elegant in this weather (whatever weather that is)?

The option with the most Grand results is to say, "Ah sure, feck it." You will, of course, give a feck if it's a first date or a fancy event, but you have zero control over the weather's effect on your look, so feck it anyway. Might as well adjust your philosophy because that's the one thing you can control: your make-up will slide off regardless.

Irish women have learned to go with the flow, weather wise. It really is best to just embrace it.

★ Embrace your face, now make-up free because a wind picked up en route and you were on your bike. Smile. *You're Grand. You don't care.*

★ Got splashed by a big, evil bus and a giant "that wasn't there yesterday" puddle? Steer the conversation round to pedestrian safety and civic courtesy: now you're doing something great for your community.

★ The worst is frizz. Ungroomed, unkempt hair,

neither straight nor curly. Awful. Again: no way to avoid it. Even on the driest day in Ireland, the atmosphere seems to have a kind of moisture memory. Step out of a professional hair salon and your hair will still be 3 inches taller by the time the door has swung shut behind you. That's just what happens here. Not a lot of shampoo commercials get made in this country. Suck it up.

Trying to stop the weather affecting your day, or even your dress sense, is futile. The key to pulling off a grand look despite the elements is to take them in your stride: put on a big smile and come up with a story about it. Stories are your best accessory: they go with everything.

Picnics in the Car

• • • • •

You feeling brave? Feck it, it doesn't matter: hopefully you're learning that you don't really need to feel brave; Grand will do. It's time to go even further from the house. It's time to go outdoors!

Picnic. The word is so cute, you'd nearly rather eat it than any of the things you're supposed to have packed for it. It conjures up idyllic images: check tablecloths, punts, potato salad, watermelon, blue skies, meadows, painted parties by the

Seine … lovely. But not here. Not in Ireland. We're now about to let you in on one of our biggest secrets. One of the things that gets us through a murky summer without giving in to one or all of the Essions. In Ireland, picnic means "meal eaten in a car while it's raining". Which, of course, it nearly always is.

Every Irishwoman worth her tiny sachet of takeaway salt knows how to rock a car picnic. We won't let bad weather deprive us of our *Déjeuner sur l'Herbe* fantasy. Or, as we know it, *Déjeuner Dans La Voiture*.

★ You might think it better to avoid hot drinks, and thereby condensation – but don't worry about it. Your breath will have fogged the windows up within about 30 seconds of parking anyway. Bring a flask of whatever you want (tea). The hotter the better. It'll be so cold outside in the freezing June air that a hot drink might be the only thing between you and death from exposure.

★ Avoid things that crumb. You can never quite get all the little feckers afterwards, and you and future owners of the car will have to relive the picnic forever. And it won't have been that great. Hard-boiled eggs = goodish (eat them quickly). Ginger nuts = bad.

★ No fancy fork food. Fingers only. Salads might work on one of your highfalutin' sunny, grassy,

happy, foreign picnics, but you need full control
here. Fork action takes up too much elbow room
and you might just end up releasing the handbrake
and, say, going over a cliff. A dramatic but plausible
possibility when …

★ … you must park at a beauty spot, even though
you will be unable to see it for mist. You must know
that it's out there somewhere. Otherwise you might
as well just have the picnic in the sauna at your
local gym. (If there are more than 2 of you in the
car, a sauna is exactly what it'll feel like. Bonus:
it's also great for the skin.)

★ Background music is allowed, but otherwise,
car picnics must be conducted in complete silence.
Overwhelmed by the sheer lack of an entire season
(summer), you'll have lost your power of speech
anyway, and a car picnic is the ideal time to really
let it sink in that you live in a country where the
government would buy a giant sunlamp – or even
borrow one for a week – if they really gave a feck
about their citizens. But they don't. You knew that
already, but a car picnic will really reinforce that
for you.

Car picnics, as stressful and miserable as they can be, are
better than no picnics at all. You must have them. And they're

ideal for a date with someone you see as a potential life partner, because if you can get through a car picnic together, there's nothing in life you can't face.

Irish Women and Salad
•••••

We have a tricky relationship with salad in Ireland. We love the idea of it, we know we should eat it, but we're genetically hardwired to repel it. The raw movement has a particularly tough time here because – as a cautious people – we like stuff cooked. "You don't expect me to eat that, do you? Do I look like a rabbit?"

Of course the weather's to blame again. It's no fun eating a soggy leaf in a torrential rainstorm. Salad isn't going to warm you up. You may as well eat it in a cold shower and throw a handful of salt in any open cuts you might have while you're at it and just really go to town on the misery.

We're not sure what salad's up to. It goes from ground to plate in 2 moves and anything that easy isn't to be trusted. It must have something to hide. When you cook food, you get to spend a bit of time with it – get to know it. Potatoes – our spuddy buddies – can't be digested unless they're cooked and they kept us alive for many years. Eating a raw potato is worse than having no potato at all. Salad is the vegetable equivalent of

a one-night stand; we're simply not convinced it's going to call us after.

For the longest time, Irish women NEVER had salad at home. You wouldn't even think of it. You got salad in hotels, usually at funerals; already in the throes of grief, you'd be given salad. On that grim, funereal plate would invariably be:

★ one hard-boiled egg
★ some sad ham
★ beetroot out of a jar
★ one really, really limp leaf of lettuce.

Just the one – you wouldn't insult people by giving them too much lettuce to deal with at such a sad time.

This "salad" is the main reason why Irish vegetarians still sometimes have to explain to relatives that ham isn't a vegetable.

Irish women do eat more salad these days. But we make sure to have it with chips. For balance.

COTTAGE INDUSTRY ALERT: If you can come up with some kind of fruit-ripener/vegetable flavour enhancer, you stand to make a lot of money. And live to a great age.

How To Be a Secret Agent (VEGETARIAN)

•••••

I'm now getting in to some really secret territory. Underground, almost, like vegetables. Much like the salads we find ourselves having to explain, vegetarians in Ireland are treated with the utmost suspicion.

With our massively lucrative beef industry, it's seen as almost unpatriotic not to eat meat. You're making a mockery of the country's progress and recent return to prosperity. You hate Ireland.

All you have to do is look at the happy farmers running around in fields in Irish meat commercials to see how bound up in Irishness meat is. It's all blissed-out animals, lush green grass and pure streams. Wasn't one of our greatest ancient legends about a bull? You're a traitor. You hate Ireland.

But secretly, many Irish women are vegetarians. We like animals and our arteries. Queen Meadbh's battle for that bull was nothing compared to a modern Irishwoman's fight to avoid meat, though.

Your only option is to become a secret agent.

It won't be easy: iMOMs and their agents are on to you. They don't want to see you deprived of meat. They're afraid that without it you'll waste away to nothing and waft off a cliff

like Peig's son. They're afraid you'll offend hosts and make fusses asking for vegetarian options – ham, for instance, when there's none in the house.

If you want to be a secret agent, ask yourself if you'll be strong enough not to crack under questioning: "Why? For animals? For health? Does it disgust you? Do we disgust you? Do you think you're American? Do you wash? Is water vegetarian? Don't you ever want to get pregnant? What about calcium – you could break a hip. You eat fish, though, yeah? Ham? No? Why? WHY? WHY??"

Now that there are more vegetarian options in Ireland than ever before, and soya lattes flow down every street, you should still take care you're not overheard ordering one.

Secret Agent Strategy:

★ Never ever say you're vegetarian. You might as well wear an "I hate Ireland" t-shirt at a St Patrick's Day parade. Better to go around beating your chest and shouting "MEAT!" occasionally, like everybody else does. This will keep you below the radar for a time.

★ A good disguise is a butcher's apron daubed in red paint. Wear this at all times.

★ When friends are choosing a restaurant and someone suggests vegetarian, or Indian or Thai

where there are tons of veggie options, roll your eyes: "But they don't serve enough MEAT! It's all broken up into pieces – you can barely see it." Irish people are very stubborn, so suggesting doing something else will make them dig their heels in and you'll soon find yourself with a lovely bowl of sticky rice in front of you.

★ Slip into restaurants earlier in the day and bribe the waiting staff. Later, you can order "the lobster – and make sure you kill it extra cruelly" without even winking at the server. They will bring you tofu in a red shell, your fiver still gleaming out of their back pocket.

★ Take a venus flytrap everywhere you go. Feed it any unwanted meat you're served.

★ If you crack and accidentally blow your own cover by ordering a superfood salad, catch yourself on quick. Say "I have to eat this. Ugh! The doctor says I'm eating too much meat. I ate so many burgers yesterday, I mooed." Make disgusted noises through every delicious, refreshing bite.

★ If anyone else orders vegetarian, bang the table and say "Traitor!" Move to the next table, humming the national anthem aggressively from behind your menu for good measure. Let some time elapse, then

follow your friend to the toilet, hug them and cry.
But check for surveillance equipment first.

This should mean you get through just about alright. But you're on your own now and we've already said too much. Good luck. This section will self-destruct in 10 meat-free seconds.

Don't Make a Fuss: How To Do Restaurants

• • • • •

Restaurants aren't Irish women's natural milieu. They're a bit too Graaahnd; they think they're great and they just don't make us very comfortable. There's too much shame that we haven't done the cooking ourselves, or haven't at least offered to bring dessert. This shame is in your genes, whether you're a total homebody or you don't know one end of a spatula from the other. This is why Irish women rarely make it to the end of a meal without bringing at least one plate into the kitchen and offering to wash it.

In terms of ordering, it can't only have been Irish women who looked on in awe as Meg Ryan ordered anything from lunch to a snack to her wedding cake in *When Harry Met Sally*: it's a triumph for feminist foodies everywhere. Here is a woman who wants it how she wants it. So that's what she asks for. Not us.

We sit in restaurants, quaking that they'll think we're making a fuss if we ask if it's possible to do something without cheese. "They'll think I'm criticising the chef. Or that I'm no craic. Or that I'm trying to take down the cheese board, one chunk of cheddar at a time."

There are many great books on assertiveness out there – there must be loads devoted just to restaurants. But this book is not about assertiveness: it's about Irish women. Here's how we do restaurants:

★ Do not complain. Even if your stir fry is frozen or your sorbet is on fire, do not say a word.

★ So you got given the wrong thing? Be grateful you got it at all. Aren't you lucky to have it?

★ If you find something crawling in your food, take the offending creature home and release it into the wild. You don't want to embarrass the restaurant by making a fuss.

★ When the server asks how everything is, be effusive – poetic, even. "Amazing! Delicious. Never before has such ambrosia touched the lips of mortals." As the server leaves, your companion will ask, "Why didn't you say something?" To which you reply: "I didn't want to upset her. She seems like a lovely girl. And she was in my class at school." The waitress deserves not to have her craic ruined. Besides, she will tell everyone you know if you make a fuss.

★ Finish every bite and leave a massive tip. Grumble your way out, smiling.

★ DO NOT let the restaurant have the opportunity of correcting mistakes. Just bad-mouth them around town.

Waiters and waitresses get the land of their lives when non-Irish people come into their restaurants. Tourists rearrange the menu, ask for add-ons and take-offs and if they don't like something they get a replacement or a refund. Idiots. Having it how they want it! Don't they know that making a fuss is about the least Grand thing you can do?

Carb Your Enthusiasm
•••••

You know how for the last few years, women all over the world have been ordered to stop eating carbs? And everyone just ate big lumps of fat instead and "it really worked!" (i.e. they lost a couple of pounds, along with every crumb of fun from their lives)? And their sweat smelled of bacon?

Yeah, well, loyal to the beef industry or no, Irish women

couldn't do that. We have an almost religious connection to carbs. We eat potatoes like they're going out of style, which ironically, keeps them in style. We have spuds with our spuds on special occasions. (Well, we do.)

Oh, and the bread! Batch loaf, soda cake, cake cake (CAKE!), soda farls ... POTATO BREAD. Need we go on? Nothing makes an Irish person's face fall quicker than the term "open sandwich". This is a cheat sandwich. It's really more of a deceitful salad, lacking the balls to just call itself by its proper deceitful name. Open sandwich? Case closed.

Putting the "Fun" in "Funeral"
•••••

All good things come to an end, and eventually, we all die. In Ireland, this is seen as a great opportunity. We won't let you go without a Paaaar-taaay! Funerals are one of our all-time favourite outings. It's a well-worn comedy phrase, but whoever wrote "putting the 'fun' in 'funeral'" must have had at least a little Irish in them.

Man, do we love death. Oh, we just love it. We don't like the fact that people go and we miss them, of course, but we've always been great at the old death. Sure, we've been only surrounded by it daily for millennia. Looking forward to a "good death" takes up a decent portion of our thinking time.

Keening was almost a part-time career for many women. Like volunteer fire-fighters or Superman, you'd be minding your own business (probably milking a cow or weaving) when you'd get the call; someone had died. You and the rest of the town's best cry-ers would be called upon to go to a funeral and wail (keen) your hearts out. The louder the wailing, the better the send-off.

Having keeners there meant everyone else could repress their unseemly emotions like normal.

•••••★•••••

COTTAGE INDUSTRY ALERT:
KEENING Keening is a skill that's been neglected too long, and something we should probably resurrect. Like most Irish women, you probably spend most of your time crying or on the verge of tears anyway, so why on earth shouldn't we be paid for it?

•••••★•••••

Traditionally, there was always a lot of other work for Irish women at funerals too. Setting out grand feeds of sandwiches and drink for the wake, mourning (pretending to like the deceased) for hours, and singing and dancing like loons made

TARA FLYNN

for hungry and thirsty work. You were supposed to pray, but most people got carried away with the chats between rosaries.

The festivities ... sorry ... *grieving* went on for 3 days with the deceased laid out in pride of place on the kitchen table. You might say "gross" but by day 3, you'd be so used to the body that you'd have to be careful not to be putting the teapot down on his head. By the time they'd take him off to be buried, you were just so pleased to get your table back that you felt an awful lot better about his passing.

Some say wakes were a form of catharsis: we say telly hadn't been invented yet, and that *Winning Streak* probably takes up a lot of the grief-slack these days.

We have death down to a fine art here in Ireland. No doubt about it: we definitely know how to put the "fun" into funeral.

LOOKING GRAND, FEELING GRAND:

Fashion, Health and Beauty

It's not that Irish women don't care how we look, it's just that we have a very particular way of dealing with it. And we definitely worry about health (i.e. the daily delaying of our inevitable demise), so feeling grand is very important. Looking Grand is a little more complex, as we've been taught it can lead to sex (which we'll deal with in the next section). Want to get that all-round, Grand glow? You've come to the right place.

A Grand Pair of Genes

There is no escaping your genes, and nowhere is this truer than in Ireland. Everywhere you go, you'll be told who you look like, or that "you would say that", or asked who you belong to – so they can go about categorising you according to ancestry. There will be some class of an opinion about you before you

even open your mouth.

Not only do Irish women evolve into our mothers, we evolve into an unavoidable, quintessential Irish shape.

You've read about the basic body types in women's magazines – mesomorphs, endomorphs, ectomorphs. Basically, no matter how much you wish it weren't so, no matter how hard you work out in defiance, you will always retain your basic body shape.

Now meet the Hibernomorphs: the shape all Irish women revert to, all things being equal. Some of us are short. Some of us are tall. We may look different to the naked eye. But underneath, we are all exactly the same shape.

Hibernomorph traits:

★ Short and squat: even if you start out tall and lean, the pressure – atmospheric and from the Essions – will eventually squish you down.

★ Broad, rounded shoulders: no amount of yoga or trying to swim away can ever undo the years of hunching over radiators or hovering over open fires for warmth. In fact, if someone were to give us a push at the top of a hill, we'd roll forward in a perfect ball and simply unfurl at the bottom.

★ Stout legs and grand thick ankles, strengthened by all the protest marches we have to go on.

★ Fists clenched from shaking them at the

television when *The Week in Politics* is on.

These are all common to every Irishwoman. There is no escape. It's your destiny, so roll with it.

Being a Grand Hoult

•••••

There are people who don't fully understand the Hibernomorph shape and unkindly stereotype Irish women as portly; hulking girls who go around with our sleeves rolled up and our arms folded, throwing people out of places. But that's simply not true. Although we remain Hibernomorphs underneath it all, Irish women come in all shapes and sizes. Some of us are really slight and have to watch out in the wind. Some of us are sturdier, and can show support by lending ballast to the slighter ones on windy days.

What is true, however, is that we all have a magic fat layer. We are what is poetically referred to as "a Grand Hoult". In other words, we haven't wasted away in a Famine and there's something to "hoult" on to. This is a massive compliment and a credit to you and your entire gene pool. You may not be able to see this magic layer on all of us, but it's there. It's a base-line of insulation, giving us a lovely warming aura – like in the old Ready Brek adverts. Being a Grand Hoult fills out a jumper just perfectly. (More on jumpers shortly.)

You can work out like a trooper, win Miss Bodybuilder

International and have a body-fat percentage of 0.001%, but being a Grand Hoult underneath it all keeps even the tiniest Irish person from looking severe.

We also enjoy eating what we like because not eating what you like is boring. Being a Grand Hoult – whatever your size – is part of the national identity.

Diets: Not Grand
•••••

Which leads us to diets, which don't work. We all know this. But nobody knows it better than an Irishwoman, because she simply will not stick to one. That brings our diet failure rate in this country to 100%. If not higher.

We have will power coming out the wazoo – but we just get bored very quickly and life's too short not to have the things we like to eat or drink. God knows, what with the bad weather and the not-supposed-to-have sex (it's coming, it's coming), we need something we can enjoy guilt-free. Don't make us feel guilty about food now too.

Besides, as far as our elephant memories are concerned, we've only just come out of a Famine. The idea of turning food down by choice so "soon" goes against our better judgement.

You've seen how we feel about salad: it's fine eating veggies all day if you live somewhere where they taste of something.

Irish vegetables in season are great: the rest of the year, they can taste like water with a bit of added fibre. There's a window of about 4 sunny weeks for them to even approach "palatable" let alone "nice". 4 weeks is not a lot of veg action, overall.

Slimming aids and replacement meal systems are a horrific thing to do to your body – especially your mouth – but the extra shipping to get them here means the horrible soups 'n 'shakes 'n' snacks cost a million euro.

And so, within reason, we eat what we like and balance it with Grand Irish activities, like being a Great Walker, which we'll explore later in this section. So eat, drink and be Irish: we may not be the best at moderation, but we will walk rings around you in the park.

What's Under the Jumper?

Luckily, there's a look that suits every Grand Hoult of a Hibernomorph. The jumper.

The jumper is intrinsic to an Irishwoman's life. They're why we don't get cold. They're a humble, lumpy fashion statement. They cover a Hibernomultitude. We always make sure there's a Grand, sensible jumper to hand. Not a "sweater" – too posh. A jumper. A pullover. A *geansaí*.

When you see us out and about in the wind and the rain,

without a care in the world, you may think it's natural hardiness. But what you don't know is that that quiet and uncharacteristic confidence comes from the fact that we're never more than 20 metres from a decent jumper. It may be in a backpack; it may be in the boot of a car; someone else may be carrying it for us, but even if it's not readily apparent, it's near. In a pinch, we'll carry a map showing all the shops in range where a jumper might be bought at extremely short notice. (There's a reason why Shaws is Almost Nationwide.) We might be knitting one under the table while we chat to you, or we may have one stowed in a phone booth, for emergency use – *SuperGeansaí* to the rescue!

MADE UP FACT #9 Since that film with Colin Farrell and the sniper, nobody uses phone booths in Ireland anymore. They're empty. This makes them the perfect place to stow emergency jumpers.

Jumpers aren't pretty. They're tough. They're thick. They're ragged round the edges. They're nothing you would look for in a man. But they not only keep us warm, they give us the only edge of confidence we may ever have.

What, you ask, about those gorgeous Aran sweaters sold

in every Irish gift shop and airport? That cost as much as the airfare that brought the tourist there? Yeah, unless we're part of a tourist welcoming committee or folk band, we don't actually wear those. Sorry.

•••••★•••••

MADE UP FACT #10 The Aran jumper was invented 1,000 years ago when a Connemara sheep swallowed a Celtic cross.

COTTAGE INDUSTRY ALERT: If you can actually make an Aran jumper, you get the freedom of every city in Ireland. These are so impossible to knit that, if you crack it, people are so in awe they feed you and give you the keys to their cars. They're so expensive that if you sell one you can pay off a pre-2008 mortgage.

•••••★•••••

The Wearing of the Green: Fashion

•••••

Along with not having great bodies, or at least not believing that we do, Irish women tend to dress for comfort or – on the off-

chance the cross nun who taught you religion in school might be passing – modesty. Practicality's an issue we're well practised in too: what with having to collect turf from the top of mountains in the rain, to always being pregnant, in terms of outfits, Irish women know how to cover up and get on with things.

If peacocks are the flamboyant ones and peahens are all drab, muted browns, then where does that leave us when Irish blokes have traditionally been happiest in grey flat caps? Most of the jewellery displayed in the National Museum is functional: we seem to have been great fans of the clasp. The famous Tara brooch is thought to have been a cloak pin whose main function was to keep cloaks closed. Maybe it was our newfound shyness at work again: maybe looking down at our own cloak adornments was easier than making eye contact with anyone else. Either way, these brooches are a lot more beautiful than a popper or a zip.

Then there was the whole having to make your own clothes situation: it's not easy to stay fashion forward when you're tethered to a loom.

There were almost no fashion magazines – or if there were, they'd probably have had the Pope on the cover: "COVERING UP IS THE NEW BLACK". No point in even asking about the suitability of miniskirts. You knew the answer. You just knew.

Somewhere around the 1980s, all that changed. We got all designery. Not just taking notice of design itself but specifically

of things designed by Irish people. Mostly men, initially, but it was a good start and paved the way for women to come. Wearing Irish became a real badge of pride and saying "I'm wearing Keogh/Rocha/Mortell" gave someone an extra reason to sashay – you were celebrating Irish design and putting money back into the economy. Hurrah! Shame that the only red carpets back then were for Mass or Papal visits, but you could still give a little twirl on your way back from communion.

GREEN: Sadly, more can't be made of our national colour, because it just isn't the easiest to wear. Green can go so wrong. If it's too mossy it's practically muddy, and you disappear – camouflaged – every time you pass a tree or high hedge. Too brash and you look like you're advertising sweet corn. So unless you really know what you're doing – or you're going for an interview to be an iMOM of the Skies – go easy on the green.

What's in Your Grandbag?

•••••

The ultimate celeb magazine question, usually accompanied by pictures of smart wallets, smart phones, tiny travel jars of ludicrously expensive creams and intact lipsticks (somehow not covered in smooshed eye pencil-with-the-cap-off, like most Irish women's bags). Irish women can't be the only ones who see these features and call "bullshit".

Here are the secrets of an Irishwoman's handbag, or Grandbag.

★ First, clutches are OUT. Not just this season, FOREVER. You have a lot of stuff you need right now plus a ton of just-in-case items. You also have a historic need to be shouldering something: turf/ milk pails/a burden. So streamlined is out.

★ Basically, what you're looking for is a large hemp sack with a shoulder strap. If you tried to carry an Irishwoman's bag dangling off the front of your arm like the reality TV stars do in magazines, it would snap off. You do not want to lose an arm, so make sure any straps are sturdy.

Then into this strappy hemp sack you put:

1. Essentials:

★ Money, some in a wallet, some rolling around in the lining. For years.

★ A key ring with keys on it, most of which you can't remember what for

★ The deeds to your home, in case you pass a bank

★ A musical instrument

★ At least 2 good books (public transport can be infrequent)

★ A hi-tech phone

★ A large hard-back diary because you "don't trust the phone"
★ An industrial size pot of Vaseline
★ Superfluous sunglasses
★ A raincoat, reflective gear, a torch, snow-grips, slip on shoes
★ A forgotten banana. You want a nice slick of that over everything.

2. Just in case:

★ A toothbrush
★ A camping stove
★ Condoms
★ An eye pencil-with-the-cap-off (soon to be smooshed, never to be found)
★ Dog treats
★ More money

If you can find anything in your Grandbag first go, you haven't packed it right. That's the reason so many bananas go under the radar only to emerge 6 months later in time for a game of "WTF did this used to be?" A Grandbag should be big enough that an onlooker might think your hopes, dreams and aspirations were inside it. Which, after all, they should be; these are essentials.

There have been attempts to get Irish women to streamline,

and minimise, and go "fashion" with their handbags, but never for long. Grandbags always win out. The best accessory an Irishwoman can have is a welt on her shoulder. A welt that screams to the world "I will never be caught out, come rain, shine, or the Apocalypse. I'm road-ready. Self-sufficient. Do not mess with me." As chic as they are, not a lot of your designer bags can deliver on that.

Grand Standing:
High Heels

•••••

Plenty of Irish women wear high heels. But they're still a bit foreign to us. We have a lot of Being a Great Walker to do and the ground here is too soft. Nothing is less elegant than walking across a bog in high heels. That's probably why heels don't feature in *Peig* very much.

Tip: If you must wear high heels, make sure you're near a sturdy wall for leaning and break-taking.

A further word of warning: we already have the grand calves of Fianna warriors. Regular heels action only makes them more pronounced. So be very careful, or your calves won't fit into anything. Like rooms.

A brogue will sort you out: in fact brogue comes from *bróg*, the Irish for shoe. Not a type of shoe, just "shoe". The concept

of shoe. All shoes. In our language, this is how a shoe should be: a grand, sturdy, round-toed, solid-soled, last-you-for-life shoe. There were no variations and you either had shoes or you didn't (mainly you didn't).

It may be hard to accept, but your cultural make-up and squished Hibernomorph shape just isn't built to support stilettos. Sorry about that.

•••••★•••••

HOW TO WALK IN MUCK:

If you live in Ireland for more than half a day, you will encounter muck. It's a particular kind of mud, that sucks. *Mud + suck = muck.*

Do not be fooled by muck's mud-like appearance: *this is no innocent mud*. The worst that can happen with mud is a bit of spattering. Dry in, brush off. Sweet. We long for mere mud.

Those quicksand pits in old silent movies had nothing on muck. With muck, no matter how sturdy the shoe or boot, it will be off before you know it, and there you'll be, standing in the muck in your socks, miserable, and realising that the only way home is squelch by squelch.

★ To minimise muck suckage: try not to let it know you're there. Tramping through heavily will only anger it. Appease it by approaching respectfully and easing through, one step at a time.
★ Heel to toe walking is no good to you now. You have to kind of hover, touch down and take off again like a mythological swan, glancing off the surface of a mythological lake.
★ Repeat til you're out of bog danger.

MADE UP FACT #11: There's a theory among made-up Irish physicists that muck is the matter that makes up black holes.* (*It isn't.) Black holes are the absence of muck. Or as we call it, "being inside".

• • • • • ★ • • • • •

Be patient. If you can't perfect the above manoeuvre (and it takes a lifetime of practice), just try and circumvent mucky areas. Even if this means you have to hire a boat. Otherwise, enjoy your squelchy socks.

A Great Walker

• • • • •

We've hinted at this a few times already: there's one thing Irish women are even better than Grand at, and that's walking. We

are Great Walkers (see below). Physical activity has always been the backbone of an Irishwoman's life. Whether it be scaling a mountain and pulling a large hemp sack up after you, heaving a cow hilariously out of a ditch, or shouldering the burden of being a nuisance to society, we're no slouches.

Even if an Irishwoman doesn't have a gym membership, she walks everywhere. To the shops, to Mass, around the kitchen while listening to Joe.

You see, it's ingrained. We don't like sitting idle. We can't. We've spent so long outdoors in the pouring rain looking for food or inspiration, it's in our genetic coding now. Besides, if ever there were a people that needed to get pre-pregnancy bodies back, it's us. Even those of us who have never been pregnant.

The cottage industry trend has spawned a load of female fitness instructors. Every park you pass has an Irishwoman barking encouragingly at another Irishwoman that SHE CAN DO IT. That's new. And spinning finally isn't only about flax anymore.

We have a bit more free time than we had and, although we realise it probably should be taken up with the traditional praying, it just hasn't worked out that way for some of us. So we work it out another way.

Exercises Irish Women Enjoy:

★ Spinning. It's very like going into town on the bike for messages long ago. We have the memory in

our legs. We love this one.

★ Swimming. We're an Atlantic island. Being able to swim not only gives you great arms but enables you to get into town during the inevitable winter flooding, or to catch up if you miss the boat to England.

★ Lifting weights. We never had to do this when we had babies on each hip. It's a wonder the Church doesn't argue against contraception by encouraging great guns.

★ Boxing. Katie Taylor. That is all.

★ Cross-country anything: running, walking, whatever you're having yourself. In times of rebellion, Irish women had to do a lot of message-carrying and hiding. A bit of difficult terrain is the kind of challenge we like.

★ Yoga. We did feel a bit guilty there for a while when Pope Benedict XVI and that priest in Donegal said it was Satanic, but Irish women love a bit of yoga. Turns out, we're pretty bendy. But we knew that – if we hadn't been, we'd have snapped in two long since.

★ Dancing. Just be careful it's not too sexy. More on that shortly.

• • • • • ★ • • • • •

A GREAT WALKER

There's one activity we love more than any other: *Walking*. And we don't want you thinking we think we're great but apparently we're the fastest at it in Europe. Everyone can do it. Everyone does it. Add a dog or drive a cow ahead of you for maximum authenticity. *Being "a great walker"* doesn't just mean you're fit, it means you're wise. It's an almost magical cure-all, reinforces our connection with the elements (muck included), banishes hangovers and is one of the main reasons for relationships lasting. Aim to have "She was always a great walker" mentioned in your eulogy at least twice, if not more. You might even want to have it on your headstone.

MARCHING

Another reason we're great walkers is that we're always having to protest against something. If Irish women didn't march every few weeks, the government would probably forget we were there. Marching is a great way to keep fit, stay visible and meet like-minded women (and men) who're cross about stuff and choose to vent it in a positive way. You may get some non-like-minded people standing on the sidelines shouting at you, but don't worry: this is great! Now you know who not to invite to your next sEssion.

••••• ★ •••••

Grand Sport

•••••

Irish women are terrifying on a pitch. Or on the sidelines wishing death to their opponents (otherwise known as supporting). We're used to being on fields in battle, you see, so no net is going to get in the way of us or our armies (otherwise known as teams).

••••• ★ •••••

BEST FANS IN THE WORLD

Irish women would win gold like Katie Taylor every single time if supporting were an event. We're the best in the world, the players are always saying it. Forget St Patrick's Day, sporting events are when we paint ourselves green (or whatever are our county colours) and go absolutely nuts on the sidelines. Believe me – as supporters, you do not want to come up against us. We will cheer your faces off.

••••• ★ •••••

The Ireland Women's Rugby team are amazing right now and we are incredibly proud of them. But hurling – the Irish game – is the fastest and most terrifying game on the planet. Too terrifying for foreigners to play: even tall, brick shithouse men are reduced to jelly by this game. It's like hockey, if hockey were played with cannons and samurai swords and jet packs, while hard things (actually a "ball" known as a "sliotar") are thrown at your face. And of course Irish women were not going to be left out of that level of craic.

When Ireland was just a new baby nation, Irish women made up *camogie*. Women's hurling. All it means, really, is that you're hurling just as athletically and throwing just as many hard things, but you're throwing them athletically at someone else who has boobs.

•••••★•••••

MADE UP FACT #12 An early name idea for camogie was "gurling". This was dismissed outright for being much too made-up.

•••••★•••••

One of the best things about *camogie* is that players play in what's called a *skort*, a shorts/skirt combo that means they're equipped for action, but still look ladylike while they puck *sliotars* at each other. We now boast some of the toughest and

most brilliant women athletes on the planet. If only they were on the telly more often. (Seriously. Skort. And you thought "gurling" was bad.)

Defuzz

Irish women removing hair is a very recent development. In the past, your thick socks would have covered your leg hairiness up nicely. Your Dress would come below the knee to meet the sock. At optimum regrowth length, there would be a delicious intertwining of sock and hair so you wouldn't quite know where sock ended and Irishwoman began.

We're not saying you must engage in hair removal: it's every woman's prerogative to be as hairy as she likes. But sometimes, defuzzing has to be done. This is depilation traditional Irish style:

•••••★•••••

★ You might have shaved a lower leg if you were, say, going to a wedding. This meant using the oldest razor you could find, preferably made by people who made biros but obviously didn't know the first thing about blades. You'd have been better off forgetting about defuzzing, and using the "razor" to write with. But if you persisted, within a few hours you'd have removed not only the unwanted hair but the top two layers of skin too. Exfoliation bonus. Nice.

★ Exhausted from doing your legs, you'd leave the hair on your underarms. This area would be covered up by some kind of wedding cardie.

★ Female facial hair was never mentioned. Bleached in secret, but never mentioned. This was lonely because – unmentioned – as far as you were concerned, no one else had it.

★ You would definitely not touch "downtown". Why would you? Weren't you after being told again and again that what lay beneath was a bit evil, so you might as well leave it covered up and warm? If you uncovered it, you'd never know what you'd unleash.

★ 'Tis far from lasers you were reared. Galaxies far, far away.

Even with South American Pope it's still not quite clear what the Catholic Church's stance on Brazilians is. But anything that brings a woman's vagina closer to the outside world must be a bad thing. So best to feel guilty about it, just in case.

Up and down the land, Irish women are getting smoother and smoother and feeling very guilty about having that much free time, we would hope. Soon it'll be almost impossible to pick us out of a line-up of women from other places.

••••★•••••

•••••★•••••

How To Get A "Lovely Colour"

•••••

If you're a woman of colour you can probably skip this next section, and we apologise for every time you've unthinkingly been told "you've a great tan". Those of us with the more traditional pasty complexion are stupid in the sun. We never see it, so we don't really know what to do when we get it. On the odd occasion when it shines in Ireland for more than a minute, we go crazy and take days off work and celebrate. Kind of like when the Irish football team scores; the occurrence is so rare, we don't want to waste it.

We KNOW we should wear factor 50 and a hat and a space suit because the sun is dangerous. Especially for our freckly arses. We're just not able. We can't resist it when it appears and

we spend all our spare cash chasing it when we have time off. And we can't shake off the saying "You've a lovely colour."

> A "lovely colour" can be anything from salmon pink to lobster red to fully peeling burn.
>
> A "lovely colour" may or may not mean you've been somewhere exotic but either way you've a bit of mystery about you.
>
> A "lovely colour" might necessitate a trip to A&E, but feck it, at least you're not pasty anymore.
>
> A "lovely colour" means we hoped the feel of sun on our skin would be like champagne. In truth, it feels like Aloe Vera.
>
> A "lovely colour" means we save money on fake tan. An Irishwoman will have tried every brand going, and can give you an on-the-spot review at a second's notice. From 10 feet away.

We know it's bad for us, but we're going to go out in the sun, and this will never change. Can we all just agree to wear sunblock? Great. Now let's get out there.

The Worry, The Worry

• • • • •

Stress is one of the biggest impediments to Irish women's Feeling Grand today. Despite our Ah Sure, Feck It attitude and knowing we will, ultimately, be Grand, Irish women are not immune to the effects of stress. In fact, with so much sorrow in our history – disease, Famine, relatives blowing off cliffs – Irish women are naturally predisposed to worry. If you can't see someone in front of you, they're probably dead and it's somehow your fault.

Worry manifests itself in frowning, whimpering, looking out of windows for more worry and watching current affairs TV before bed. We all do it. We know it's not good for us, but sometimes it's unavoidable.

What Irish women realise is that not all worry is created equal. Despite having much bigger things to worry about, there are some small things you need to worry about, while some are just not worth your time or already overworked sweat glands.

WORTH WORRYING ABOUT	NOT WORTH WORRYING ABOUT
The environment. We can't take any more storms.	How you look. Learn a song instead.
Whether your elderly neighbours are OK	The government. They're all the same.
Not being a dick	Hell. We might enjoy the heat.
Equality	People who enjoy aggro
Health	Love handles
Animal welfare	Gluten
Education	Etiquette
The future	The future

40 Day Annual Detox
(OPTIONAL)
· · · · ·

Health is of course worth worrying about. And true health is not just about avoiding illness: it's peak health you're after. You want to be the best Grand rosy-cheeked woman you can be, with a spring in your step and a twinkle in your eye and all the rest of it. Detoxes have recently become the cool way to shed a few pounds, shift a few zits and generally feel self-righteous and smug.

No one enjoys feeling smug like an Irishwoman does when

she's doing her annual cleanse, or as we call it – Lent. Even if you're not religious, this Church-sanctioned, 40-day detox has been every Irishwoman's secret weapon for years. We may not diet, but we love feeling smug. We so rarely get to, you see.

HOW IT WORKS: You give up something you like for 40 days, for Jesus. Except on St Patrick's Day. On St Patrick's Day you can go nuts on chocolate or brandy or lard; you can even go nuts on nuts, if that's your poison.

40 (well, 39, shh) days later, you break this fast feeling really good about yourself, knowing Jesus is proud of you too.

So keep your juice fasts and retreats: our way is easy, doable by almost everyone and it also saves you a few quid. Even heathens can get down with that.

Beauty Routine: A Grand Glow

We may not traditionally be known as sexy, but we're handsome women all the same, God bless us. You're probably wondering how we do it. Well, ta-da! Here's our daily routine.

1. Rise at a decent hour, when you're told, like a good girl. You'll earn yourself some "knowing your place" brownie points this way. This will give you an attractive glow.

2. Make the tea for everyone else, then have one yourself, sure why not. But no sugar for you.

3. When everyone has left, it should still be early enough to splash your face with the morning dew. Splash it straight off the grass, or set up a dew collector system direct to your bathroom (if you're allowed by your husband).

4. Moisturise. Moisturise. Moisturise. Don't bother with fancy creams: whatever you have in the fridge will be Grand. You don't want to waste the butter wrapper.

5. If all that hasn't woken you up properly, go for a Grand long walk in the rain. This should dislodge any insects that were trapped in the dew or attracted to the butter.

6. Still a bit groggy? Throw in a bit of self-flagellation: even if you haven't sinned lately, better safe than sorry. This stimulates endorphins, which make everyone look awesome.

7. Once a week, go for a sauna at your local health club, if you have one. Don't tell anyone, though,

and definitely don't take any of your clothes off. Yes, you'll be roasting, but it's only your facial pores you're worried about here. Don't go mad.

8. For a special treat, get yourself a fake tan. You won't need to exfoliate first because you'll be plenty smooth after all the self-flagellation. Then paint on some creosote left over from the fencing – taking care not to blend and making sure to leave lots of streaks – OR get a professional to do it. Then you can have all the unblended streaks you like and none of the blame.

9. No need to worry about wrinkles. Your conscience is so clear from all the obedience that you won't develop many. Also, we don't have enough sun. When you see wrinkles on a pre-Peig phase Irishwoman, it's probably an allergic reaction to creosote.

10. Go to bed early (you've an awful lot of tea to make in the morning) but RAGIN'.

Beauty Sleep: Go To Bed Ragin'

•••••

People often talk about how fresh Irish women look. Sticking rigidly to the above beauty regime helps. But one of the most

important elements of that regime is getting not just the right amount of beauty sleep, but the right <u>kind</u>.

The most heated live current affairs programmes on Irish television air late at night, after kids have gone to bed; during these shows you'll hear parents using the kind of language you wouldn't even hear at an All-Ireland final between Dublin and Cork. No child should ever hear what we say about our politicians.

However, there's a wonderful catharsis (and we can never have too much of that) to watching this shit before bed: you turn the air blue, throw things at the telly, tweet something obnoxious using the show's hashtag, yawn, stretch, brush your teeth and turn in. You get all that junk out, right there in the living room so it never even makes it up the stairs to trouble you further. Trust me, you'll sleep like a Grand big Irish baby.

Grand Make-Up

•••••

Now you know how to achieve a Grand inner glow, there'll still be times when you have to make some kind of extra effort. Irish women split into several make-up camps:

Air hostess: The iMOM of the Skies, this woman applies make-up with a trowel. How thickly? If you can get your make-up to enter a room about 30 seconds before you do, you've

got it just about right. Team with a block hair colour too dark for your skintone, and you're onto a winner. Once you find a lip colour you like stick with it. Do not update it. Ever. A frosted '60s lip – while deeply unflattering – will never go out. Make sure there is enough make-up on your neck to come off not just on your collar, but to hang in the surrounding air after you leave. Ditto fragrance. Buy it Duty Free at the airport, in industrial drums. It should have a name like "Unique" or "Foreign" or "Why Not?" Forget chemtrails, this is what jets actually leave in their wake.

Nun: Clue's in the name – none. No make-up. It's sinful. Carry a spit-hanky in your sleeve to wipe it off everyone else. Pull their socks up while you're at it.

Druid: The Druid woman always looks naturally beautiful. Unlike the Nun, she does wear make-up sometimes, but in earthy natural tones like "Moss", "Moonbeam" or "Muck". Her skincare routine is bathing in a natural spring; dew is her moisturiser. Her hair falls in glorious waves down her back, as if the Little People themselves saw to any split ends while she slept. Druids are often offered modelling contracts, but they turn them down because all the travel would take them too far from their spring.

Mass-cara: A lot of Irish women fall into this category. You go make-up free a lot of the time (it'd all slide off in a hot

kitchen/office/during labour anyway). But you will lash on a lip and an eye for special occasions, such as Mass.

Celtic Tigress: This look stuck around even after all the cosmetics money went away in 2008. Tigresses have long, straight, glossy hair, and tattoo everything on: eyebrows, eyeliner, smiles. This perma-make-up somehow makes them look taller. They have identikit teeth that they got on the internet, perfect skin from all the resurfacing, and they've seen more laser action than Luke Skywalker. Their cosmetics all come in one shade: "Expensive". It's marketed in tiny pots with ingredients like crushed-up pearls, gold vapour and angels' tears. How any remaining Tigresses are continuing to fund this look since the recession is unclear.

Stepford Mammy: iMOMs can come in any of the above categories, but there is one special one for the new kind of supermammy we mentioned earlier who thinks everyone should be an iMOM so long as they were born women and *go to Mass at least once a week*. The look is soft-focus, as if they somehow managed to slick a film of Vaseline over your eyes before they came in. They wear make-up so incredibly subtle and perfect it may have been applied by a robot. The idea here is to look perfectly groomed, but as if you didn't spend too much time on yourself; time spent preening = less time praying. Products include: "Holy Smoky Eyes", "Immaculips"

and "L-Ash Wednesday". ("Burning Bush" was discontinued for being a bit too raunchy.) They wear pearls at the neck, but nothing as showy as lip gloss. Unless they're on TV. But then they're not one bit happy about it, so they purse their lips a lot in protest.

There is, of course, crossover: I mean, who hasn't had a Nun day? But broadly, we all fall into one category or another. So have fun experimenting, and decide, just like the characters in *Sex and the City*: which one are you?

●●●●● ★ ●●●●●

MAKE-UP: THE LINE

Whichever of the above make-up categories you belong to, there's one unifying belief: *never, ever blend*. Irish women pride themselves on The Line. It's like a national trademark.

Having done a great make-up job, you're going to want people to know where your face ends, and your neck begins. You've paid for the make-up, and you want people to know you've got it on.

Necks don't need make-up, they're necks, and usually hidden in modest collars or scarves. If they're not, they should be.

How to do The Line:

1. Choose a foundation at least 2 shades up or down from your own skin tone. Wait: two? Don't let us limit you. Go as many shades contrast as you like. The whole idea is that it looks like your face and neck came from two different people.

2. Draw a sharp line from ear to ear, following your jaw line. Do it in pencil, if you're scared, but really, you'll want to go ahead and mark it out in indelible ink: you'll be doing this every day for the rest of your life.

3. No make-up below The Line

There you go. Off you go into the world. Everyone will know that you're Irish by your utter disdain for everything below the neck i.e. *awesome*.

• • • • • ★ • • • • •

COTTAGE INDUSTRY ALERT: FACE-HOOD

A kind of hood that covers the head and neck but leaves the face exposed, allowing Irish women to focus on the face part and achieve a nice, sharp line without having to worry about blurring. (No, it's not a balaclava.)

• • • • • ★ • • • • •

7

GRAND
SEX

★

And so, we come to what is really the main event. Irish women's biggest secret and one of the reasons you might have put on Grand make-up in the first place. This is the big key; unlock this secret, and you're unlocking much of the rest of what's going on with Irish women. SEX. It's a tricky word for us, only just emerging as we are from generations of being told that S-E-X equals S-I-N. This goes against everything our grand pagan hearts used to know, but forgot somewhere along the way while we were being shushed. This tug between wild pagan nature and knowing our sexual place has wreaked havoc. Now maybe our underlying contrariness will make a little more sense. Things are getting better, and Ireland is returning somewhat to its roots as a sex-positive place to be, although we're not quite there yet. So, SEX. What are our sex secrets? How do Irishwoman do "it"?

Nudity

• • • • •

The safest rule of thumb for this one? AVOID IT. Irish women are very rarely naked. Even under our clothes. We used to be naked all the time, in ancient times: we loved it! But as soon as we heard it was a sin we covered ourselves up and stayed that way.

Playboy was illegal here til about 5 minutes ago. That was way too much skin for people to handle in a newsagent's only a few feet from the stack of *Ireland's Own*s. There's only ever been one Irishwoman in *Playboy* as far as we know. German *Playboy*, luckily, so there was little chance of the relatives seeing it. Thank goodness she was on a beach so if one of the relatives did see it, it could be explained to them as an over-enthusiastic Christmas swim.

Nudey women in Ireland are ridiculously problematic. There's the shame, of course: a naked woman is almost definitely about to do something disgustingly sexy, and the response of the onlooker will be that nudey woman's fault. The Irish word for "fine", "*breá*", is pronounced "bra", so every Irish secondary school essay involving a fine day becomes the most hilarious thing a teenage boy has ever heard. Imagine the hilarity when actually confronted with an *actual bra*, let alone the removal of one.

★ If you really, really have to get naked – changing into a sensible swimsuit, for example – and you're

away from a lead-curtain-lined cubicle, there is something you can do. Be a ferret (see instructions overleaf). Irish women could get Olympic gold at changing into a sensible swimsuit under a towel. The swimsuit *must* be sensible and you must change under a towel for the following reasons:

★ It's going to be cold. You will have blue arms and legs, anyway. Why get a blue anything else?

★ You aren't the only person on the beach. You might give some poor person – who's already in shock at having to have their picnic inside the car – the fright of their lives.

★ Spare a thought for any tourists present, who really can do without the prospect of snow blindness, dazzled as they will be at their first glimpse of Irish skin, au naturel.

All you need for this technique is a large beach towel and don't forget: plenty of shame.

••••• ★ •••••

THE SHAME, THE SHAME

It can't be stressed too often: always, *always* be ashamed of your body. If you really want to be an Irishwoman, you must spend most of your waking

hours (and many of your sleeping ones) in a resolute state of shame.

If you're already a bit dissatisfied with how your body looks, great; you've got a head start. Someone who likes how they look naked might forget to be ashamed and put on the extra jumper.

Being ashamed of being a woman is a great starting point: we have lots to be ashamed of, having caused most of Ireland's grief by populating the place non-stop, all by ourselves, and by leading blokes into sin with our sinful bodies (jumpers notwithstanding).

★ Disgrace is another thing to think about: unlike shame, which is inbuilt, disgrace is avoidable. You never want to hear "You're a disgrace to me/this house/the parish." You will hear them, though, if you are out of the house long enough. Best to stay in, in as chaste a jumper as possible.

●●●●●★●●●●●

HOW TO BE A FERRET

You don't really want to be an actual ferret: hunted for sport and with a face like a ... well, ferret. But you will have to make like one if you ever want to

go for a swim on an Irish beach. You will need:

1. A giant towel. You may even choose to sew together a kind of beach poncho where you pop the whole thing over your head. There is very little skill involved in this, though. You can do better than that.

2. A second pair of elbows. These may be imaginary, but this is how your swimsuit-wrangling should appear to an onlooker. To clarify, it should look as if – under your towel – you've released some fighting ferrets and you're attempting to retrieve them with your bare hands and maybe even convince them to mate.

3. No real ferrets.

The ferret-wrestling technique will get you more odd looks and call far more attention to your naked-underneath situation than quickly and quietly changing without ceremony. But don't try and argue that point. This is something we have always done. Get practising.

• • • • • ★ • • • • •

Not Sexy

•••••

There are some very attractive Irish people, like yer aforementioned woman in German *Playboy*, but it's not how we're generally perceived. Largely because we've learned to hide our bodies under jumpers or behind cattle or trees, where available. But the truth of the matter is that when an Irish person takes their clothes off, it's less like tantalisingly revealing the beautiful gift of your naked body … it's more like unwrapping uncooked chicken. It's not that we're not sexy – we're afraid of getting salmonella off each other.

Toplessness, even momentary toplessness, spied somewhere it's hard to avoid, like the changing room at the gym, elicits gasps and red faces – even if you haven't accidentally wandered into the men's. Try it at the beach (without a German photo crew) and you could well find yourself being discussed at length behind your back. Worse, you could be denounced by your parish for disgracing them in "acting all European". 'Tis far from that you were reared.

How To Wear The Dress

•••••

There's really only one choice of outfit for a traditional Irishwoman, covering her shameful nudity, good girl herself: The Dress. Even if your innate boldness bursts out of you by

accident, people are likely to be a lot more forgiving if you're wearing The Dress.

The Dress is a great way to show off those grand, thick Irish ankles and that bit of leg-stubble you missed without showing too much. It shows you made an effort, you have a modicum of self-worth (though not too much; be careful not to think you're great) but you're still demure and sweet and you wouldn't be talking back or anything. Even if you do, The Dress will fool them into thinking you haven't.

Here's what we're after in a Grand Dress:

•••••★•••••

THE GRAND DRESS

★ The kind of dress you'd wear to Mass. In the '50s
★ It's loose
★ It has flowers on it
★ Definitely below the knee
★ Buttons or a brooch on the front to distract from the fact that there might be another "b" word (a bra, or worse, breasts) in there.
★ That said, never forget: accessories are icing, but your dress is the cake. Don't go overboard.
★ Meryl Streep would have worn it in a film
★ An outfit in England or a magazine or somewhere might "take you from day to evening,

with just the addition of a simple belt, some earrings and attitude." Your dress should be able to take you from milking parlour to cake sale and back again. On your bike. Knees together, now.

•••••★•••••

The Dress is a lovely way to show that you're still connected to old, Romantic Ireland and therefore marriageable. The Dress makes you look like you might need a gentleman's help into a carriage or to be carried over a puddle. Perhaps most importantly, it makes you look like a *lady*.

•••••★•••••

Being a Lady

★ The female equivalent of being called a "gent", being a *lady* is one of the top Irish compliments.

★ You earn it in return for a good deed or favour, e.g. "Thanks for the homemade jam. You're a lady!"

★ Ladies speak in soft voices and say "thank you" all the time, especially if someone else is speaking and they want them to stop. Take note: this is NOT rude because they didn't raise their voices or say "shut up".

★ Ladies smile. All the time. Even if they burn their fingers on a straightening iron. Their hair is very straight.

★ Ladies can even ride a bike while wearing a dress (obvs) without parting their legs or showing their knees. It's really kind of terrifying.

★ Ladies never think about sexy times. (At least, that's what they'd like you to think.)

••••• ★ •••••

Of course, not all dresses are created equal in this regard. Some are fitted and show your shape. We're not after that effect at all. Leave that to Hollywood and Eurovision winners. That's what a lady would do, anyway.

How To Be a Great Burd

•••••

There is a kind of anti-lady who almost never wears The Dress. But let's be clear: although she's not a lady, this woman is something almost as good. She is a *Great Burd*.

Granted "bird" isn't the least sexist epithet in the world. But at least the intention is good.

••••• ★ •••••

WHAT MAKES A GREAT BURD

★ A great burd is an Irishwoman who's one of the lads.

★ She likes a pint.

★ She'd laugh if she fell in some muck.

★ She is the very definition of "sound".

★ She might have worn The Dress to her debs, but that's about it. Chinos all the way. This does not make her any less of a lady-burd.

★ Great burds are the least objectified of the women known to the men who use the term.

★ She's decent skin. A pal.

★ You would never have a one-night stand with a great burd; if you did, you'd risk the wrath of your entire gang of pals. And Irish blokes would never risk being shunned by the pals. They're just not as used to shunning as women are.

Every now and again, the friendship between a great burd and one particular pal will deepen, and they will start nesting, and maybe even have chicks. These are perhaps the greatest Irish love stories of all. The weddings are certainly the only time outside of an international sporting event when you see adult Irish males cry in public.

And guess what? Deep down, all Irish women are great burds.

Irish Women Don't Date

• • • • •

Now you've the Grand Dress on you, the right kind of Grand make-up for your type (see Looking Grand, Feeling Grand), and aware of whether you're a Lady or a Burd, you probably want to show yourself off and maybe put yourself in the way of some compliments (which you know to expertly deflect). Well, I have some bad news. Irish women don't date.

It's a wonder we ever bred, let alone as successfully as we did here in Ireland, because Irish women *do not date*. No matter how Americans in films moan about how hard dating is, they should try to get a relationship going, or even get a shift, when dating isn't part of the culture. It's so uncomplicated for them: they see someone they like in the cafeteria and walk right up to them and ask if they would like to go on a date. JESUS! *Scarle'*. They might think you were an eejit or something. On what planet is that Grand? *Jesus*.

Irish people can't be giving anyone else the soot of knowing they like them. Even if it's just a casual lust thing, you can't say it straight out: we favour the use of a complex system of signs, clues, hints and hilltop bonfires.

Basically, Irish people have to hope to bump into each other, fall over and somehow mutually instigate touching. This, even if they've been married for quite some time.

That's why matchmaking, like in Peig's time, was actually great. The match was much less likely to back out of the deal once they were in your house, talking to your father about cows. But what if you don't have a cow?

There's a reason dating coaches didn't really get anywhere in Ireland. "Why not get out of your comfort zone and try and meet someone in, say, an art gallery?" Irish people don't like to approach others unless we're a bit drunk and it's dark. Galleries are way too well lit. It just doesn't work.

There's the old joke about the Irish man who used to eat his dinner out of a drawer so he could close it quickly if someone called, and they would never know what he had. That's just the bit o' dhinner … Imagine how much more closely guarded we are with our emotions.

And so dating – actually approaching someone else and admitting that you think they're worth getting to know better – may never catch on in Ireland. But sometimes, you have to be brave. Sometimes, you see someone at a dance, or at work, or at a funeral and just can't help yourself asking…

Do You Want To Be Buried with My People

• • • • •

This is important, because traditional rules state that if you're not already a wife, you will definitely want to be one, one day.

It's the tip-top destiny of an Irishwoman. And our inability to date is a serious impediment to this.

So how do you get someone to notice you? How do you get them to commit? How do you get them to ask "Do you want to be buried with my people?"

This is the traditional Irish stuff that'll get that Claddagh ring on your finger in no time.

★ Be comely. You may let your shawl slip off your shoulders a bit if it's warm, but don't make a meal of it.

★ Have creamy skin, hair like a raven's wing, the strength of 20 men, an adeptness for the spinning wheel, a beautiful singing voice and a big dowry (at least one cow). No one in Ireland has ever met this description, but we have to have goals.

★ Be strong and feisty with your lover's opponents, but meek and obedient at home.

★ Do not let on you have your own place to live: you must seem rescuable. Besides, keeping your place will mean you'll have somewhere to go if it all goes pear-shaped.

★ Put your intended *faoi gheasa* (under a binding spell) like Gráinne did Diarmaid. People still talk about Diarmaid and Gráinne today. Spells and curses might be cheating, and some might question

whether they even work at all, but it's that or die alone. Take your pick.

★ Cook. Cook during courtship like you've never cooked before and like you never intend to cook again. Except at The Christmas.

★ Bike secret messages to and from an organisation of your intended's allegiance. This brought a lot of people together in the old days.

★ Be a teacher. Teachers are almost iMOMs already. Great marriage material.

★ Be apolitical.

★ Sing. This one is worth repeating. Harp – as ever – optional.

★ Learn how to catch and kill your own food. Very handy in a recession. And – if telly's anything to go by – very "in".

You're welcome. We look forward to being invited to your wedding.

Grand and Romantic

• • • • •

This is very tricky territory, because post-shushening, Irish women have become very suspicious. You know what we're like with compliments? Well, gifts only make us wonder what

you have to apologise for. You must have done something really bad. Basically, any romance must be some kind of trap. We just don't buy it. We want to like it but it makes us uncomfortable, like having an allergy to flowers or kittens.

We love chocolate and flowers but if the response you were after was a warm and loving one, think again. You're more likely to get "Feck off out of that, you eejit!" and an accompanying puck in the arm.

$$\bullet\bullet\bullet\bullet\bullet\bigstar\bullet\bullet\bullet\bullet\bullet$$

A PUCK IN THE ARM

If an Irishwoman really likes you, she will eventually puck you. And when an Irishwoman pucks you, you'll know you've been pucked.

A puck is probably best described as an affectionately furious kind of punch, like a reverse negging of the upper arm. We typically start pucking in our teens, and we don't stop once we mature.

Pucking is the ideal way to deflate any too-mushy-for-comfort moments while maintaining close physical contact with the object of your affection. You would never puck someone you didn't like: that's assault.

MADE UP FACT #14 Pucking may be a throwback to Viking times, where there was a lot of plundering and pillaging going on, which would have made us super cross. But once we got to know them, we noticed that Vikings were rides. Pucking may have been a way to signal interest while also indicating "Don't mess with me, Sven: I'm an Irishwoman." And Sven nursed his bruised arm with a smile. She liked him.

★★★★★ ★ ★★★★★

Here are a few more ideas for how to be grand and romantic when wooing an Irishwoman, while getting around the suspicion and discomfort.

★ Deliver any gifts in a throwaway manner, or with a caveat or task attached. Say "I got you some flowers there" but leave them outside. The extra hassle will put her at ease and she will be delighted when she comes back in out of the rain with her bouquet.

★ Take her for dinner, but make it seem like a surprise. Make sure she's not in any way appropriately dressed for the restaurant you're going to. That way, she can feel uncomfortable for

the entire meal. This will be much more familiar to her than being waited on hand and foot like the Queen of Sheba.

★ If you can get the cuisine completely wrong, even better: a steak restaurant when she's been a committed vegetarian all the time you've known her, for instance. You get to show her you wanted to take her out without having to pretend you've heard a word she's ever said. Paying too much attention will only put her off.

★ Chocolates. Obviously, eat half of them. The good half.

★ Valentine's Day in Ireland can be a particular minefield, as St Valentine himself is buried in a Dublin church. So, Irish women have actual empirical evidence that romance is dead. Best to ignore it altogether.

On the positive side, here are some ideal, non-suspicious ways to romance an Irishwoman:

1. Bring her tea in bed. As we know, tea makes everything OK.
2. Ask her if she's done something new with her hair. Do NOT say it looks nice, just leave the observation hanging, short of an actual compliment.

3. Pump up her bicycle tyres. She'll know.

4. Come home at the time you've said you would. Irish women are terrible worriers and, if you're late, as far as she's concerned you are definitely dead. Don't be surprised if, when you get home, there's a full-blown wake already underway.

5. Ask "Did you get that in Penneys?" if she has a new top on.

6. Offer to go out in the weather to get her something. She may be a great walker, and hardy, but sometimes the fire is nice.

7. Plan an unexpected outing – like emigrating to Boston. Not only will a change of scene work wonders for your relationship but increased job prospects will probably take a lot of pressure off you both.

8. Be foreign. No, don't act foreign, that's racist. If you're Irish, you're Irish and there's no escaping it. And why would you want to? But there's no doubt that Irish people feel foreigners are more capable of romance. Possibly because of 7.

9. Flirt with someone else. It may earn you a well-deserved puck, but by showing her you're not stuck you'll let an Irishwoman know you really, really want to be with her.

10. Leave her little notes around the house. Things like "We're out of milk" or "Couldn't find the cat – left her in" or "I have your wallet." These not only show you remember she exists, but because you're out, probably dead, now she has a bit of paper to remember you by.

11. Buy her health insurance. She would never buy it for herself.

Getting the Ride

•••••

At some point, even Irish women get to have sex. When we were still goddesses, we could admit to riding all around us, or wanting to, and it was Grand. There was no shame at all. Now you give one blowjob at a festival and you're derided all over the internet.

••••• ★ •••••

MADE UP FACT #15 In Pagan Times, the Blow Job Festival was one of the best attended of the social calendar.

••••• ★ •••••

Post-goddess era, riding became sinful and you would never admit to doing it. But with babies being born every day, someone finally had to admit that Irish women were having sex

and probably enjoying it, which was worse than having the sex in the first place.

Irish women *love* the ride. We've had to navigate so many obstacles to get to the ride (no dating, no contraception, the whole Hell thing) that by the time we actually get down to it, we're well up for it. We mean business. We've been thinking about it for a long time and we know what we want. Good luck!

•••••★•••••

FAMILY UNPLANNING: CONDOM TRAIN

Too close to the end of the sexual revolution for it not to be embarrassing, a brilliant group of Irish women went to Belfast on the "contraceptive" train and defiantly brought condoms home to the Republic. This caused a massive to-do, and contraceptives remained illegal here until the '80s, when they were still frowned upon by the Church: you could tell because the clergy led by example, forgoing contraception and spawning loads of children themselves. A quick roll in the hay wouldn't affect the next 18 years of the life of a man of God. He'd simply be moved to another parish. And he wouldn't be too worried about AIDS either; that was other people's lookout.

So here's our grateful salute to those condom train pioneers. Not only are those women heroes, it's hard not to picture a condom train as a latex bullet with a tiny sperm driver in a hat.

HOW TO BE INVISIBLE

Termination of pregnancy is illegal in Ireland. That doesn't mean Irish women don't face the difficult personal dilemma of abortion, they just have to do it abroad. Twelve women leave the island every single day for this reason. Still certain quarters proclaim that "there is no abortion in Ireland!" So a lucky 12 women a day get to be in the magical position of being completely invisible. Who knew you just had to get on a ferry to do it? Take that, Harry Potter.

••••• ★ •••••

How To Do Grand Sex
•••••

So that's our attitude to the ride, but what about the nuts and bolts, so to speak? The truth is that no matter how much you try and claim it only came in with *Dallas*, Irish people have been having sex for absolutely ages. Many of them women. So how does an Irishwoman actually do "it"?

Sin, sin, sin, sin, sin, sin, sin: even thinking about sex was a sin. Protecting yourself from pregnancy and sexually transmitted diseases was an even bigger sin. In other words, IT WAS A MASSIVE TURN-ON.

That's just taking cis-gendered, straight women into account; remember homosexuality was only decriminalised in 1993. Imagine how hot the doubly forbidden sex must have been for women attracted to women. HOT. Illegally hot.

Before St Patrick came along, we were all riding away with gay abandon. Literally. Whomever and whenever you wanted. Was it the snakes? It seems to have all gone downhill when they slithered off. Stupid, sexy snakes.

But we are where we are and despite all the obstacles, we still manage to have some grand sex. Here's a grand checklist for making with the sexy times:

★ Don't. (Yes, this again.) It makes it so much
hotter when you eventually do.
★ When you do it, try not to enjoy it. Remember
that sex is hard work, and possibly the very first day
of your new life as a mother. Forever.
★ If must be done in a bed. With the lights out.
Don't be looking at each other, ye'd only enjoy it.
★ Men sleep with women and women sleep with
men. Got it? But priests do what they like.

★ These man/woman couples <u>must</u> have babies on their minds. Ireland: the only country in the world where thinking about children during sex is the least perverted option.

★ No toys. Unless they're for the baby which is the sole goal of your union. Put a teddy on the nightstand to keep yourself on track. Stupid, sexy teddy.

★ Try and be at least a little drunk before, during and after, even if it's on too much tea. The caffeine buzz will mean you won't have to even remember whether you enjoyed it or not. And in confession, you can say you don't remember if you enjoyed it or not, without lying to a priest. Score.

★ No contraception. We've been through this. If you already have enough children (and you don't), use a complicated system involving calendars and a full chemistry lab beside the bed. It sounds awful but it's SUPER HOT.

★ Never refer directly to sex. It's riding, flaing, or whatever you're having yourself. If you do refer to S-E-X, whisper it, and make damn well sure you're ashamed of yourself, young lady.

★ Never, ever, pleasure yourself. Fingers are for counting down the days til you next ovulate.

★ Erotica has no place in Ireland, especially for

women. But feck that, we've written some for you.
(See Irotica.)

Of course things are changing here. Our wild, sexy nature could only stay submerged in shame for so long. In fact, at the moment, our attitude to sex is speeding up at a rate you might say was climactic. We're catching up with the rest of the world, from behind, in a giant orgasmic rush. Stupid, sexy Ireland.

Grand Dancing

•••••

Very few Irish women feel Grand when public motion is required. But dancing can lead to sexy times while skipping the whole asking-each-other-out-on-a-date thing we're so uncomfortable with.

Riverdance has a lot to answer for.

1. It updated Irish dancing.

2. It rejuvenated the tourist industry.

3. It's single-footedly responsible for everything good that's happened in Ireland since, understood BUT ....

4. It crash-landed us back to being comely and rocking it at the crossroads. No harm, really, since this is probably what we should have been aspiring to.

Note: not all Irish women Irish dance. In fact, with all we've got going on, it's hard to find the time to bust any kind of move. There's more to Irish dancing than Irish Dancing:

• • • • • ★ • • • • •

IRISH DANCING: Far from the glamour of *Riverdance*, many of us paid our embarrassing dues doing hornpipes on the backs of lorries at fairs in the summer and in freezing halls in winter. A hornpipe is nowhere near as sexy as it sounds, believe me. Leaping up and down in psychedelic dresses, capes a-flapping, white socks starched directly onto pink legs, ringlets scorched into existence and toes pointed hopefully towards America, this was a rite of passage for many young Irish women. Nobody really liked the music, which usually came from an old, bockety LP or an old, bockety gentleman. With this as our first taste of dance, no wonder we're not world-renowned.

BALLET: The National Ballet company (founded by Corkwoman Joan Denise Moriarty) was a miracle, given the sparse funding and the country's ambivalence to dance. But there was no job security in it and no Mars Bars, so it didn't appeal to too many Irish girls.

DISCOS: Often pronounced "Dishco", our first taste of these would have been at school, so obviously they were about anything other than

dancing, they were about snogging and attempting to smuggle alcohol in. If there was even a hint of chemistry between a shuffling pair, they were made to dance at nun's arm length, as she'd shove her upper body in between them.

For flavour, once the dancing's done, the gentle percussion of empty cider cans rolling up and down the top deck of the bus mingles poignantly with the smell of fresh vomit.

BALLROOM OF NO-DANCE: In the 1950s and '60s, dances were the only place where men and women could touch. They definitely wouldn't be doing it at home. The men would line up on one side of the hall, the women on the other. Then the long, slow walk across – across the floor, across time – to ask your intended to dance. Remember, this was pre-TV, so there was no sex. If we're to believe what we were told, it seems all that repression led to zero exploding chemistry on the dancefloor, to everyone going straight home afterwards, alone, and to nobody at all shagging each other senseless in a field. Nope. No way.

CÉILÍ: Going even further back, céilí dancing was the kind that filled the parish halls. Local musicians

would play and everyone would dance set dances together like *The Siege of Ennis* and *The Walls of Limerick*. Basically it had to have a town name and some kind of military connotation. You know, so you wouldn't be thinking about sex.

It's alleged that priests were the ones who suggested that – instead of throwing their arms up over their heads in a kind of joyous fashion, like they do in Scotland – Irish men and women keep their hands by their sides. Arms up was just too sexalicious. So it's the Church's fault that Irish dancing is so weird, with the legs flailing around all on their own down there.

FESTIVAL FREESTYLE: At summer festivals, no one sits. There's not one ass on the grass. Our inner pagans come out and we go nuts. Forget topping up your lipstick, powdering your nose, or dancing around your handbag – we dive in head first til you can't see us for sweat and muck.

• • • • • ★ • • • • •

Dance like no one is watching? We always had somebody watching. We found a way to dance anyway.

Grand Online

• • • • •

Seeing as we don't date in real life, Irish women are very sceptical altogether about dating online. There's certainly loads of potential for disaster, so who'd blame us, really?

The main problem with online dating in Ireland is that you know half the lads on there anyway.

Not used to dating, now forced to meet someone IRL (In Real Life), we get fierce sweaty. The sheer nerves of having to show your hand, to admit that you're single and might want something to happen, it's very uncomfortable for us. So we sweat – some of it intentional, in the hope of creating a kind of force field of perspiration to make us impervious to rejection.

Sometimes that same Irish resilience works against us: the date doesn't go well, but the other person's sweat-barrier shields them so they don't even realise it. "We had such a great time! Let's definitely do this again!" – when you've been counting the minutes until it's polite to invent a dying relative and leave. Irish women are just too nice to say it. We may be thinking all kinds of horrible things:

What is up with that shirt?

I think I'm allergic to his aftershave. "Muck Pour Homme".

No, I don't believe in Creationism, but I will lie! I had a great time! We should definitely do this again! I want to die!

Rather than make someone feel as bad as we feel about ourselves, we will go on 7 or more further dates before either faking our own deaths or ending up marrying the lad. It's just easier.

The best way to put people off before the dreaded IRL meet is to be honest. No one likes an Irishwoman who says what she actually thinks; you couldn't trust someone like that.

Here are a few of the kind of profiles you might come across. Don't use these, though. They're much too attractive.

> **Username**: Deirdre of Sorrows
> **Hobbies**: Sighing, Eastern European cinema, lying down, walking
> **Star sign**: Doomed
> *Hi, my name's Deirdre and I just want a laugh, really. I hate my job and my life and Ireland itself. God, it's a kip. I was going to go to America but I ended up staying due to not being bothered. I'm looking for someone who's a laugh, really, and who likes to have a laugh too. I've been single for ages. Nobody gets me. Do you?*

> **Username**: keepthefaith21
> **Hobbies**: Praying, wearing pearl necklaces, keeping tabs on other people's sex lives, abstaining from everything, walking
> **Star sign**: God

Hellooooo! I think you're lovely and I haven't even met you yet. LOL! That's how excited I am about meeting new people and finding out all about what makes them tick. I like sunsets, kittens, Mass, white tablecloths, Easter, singsongs and being offended. I'm a virgin, but don't let that put you off because
I'm great craic, LOL, and I'm looking for a husband. If you're the kind of fella who can show a girl a good time like fine dining on prawn cocktail, letting me do all the housework and picking and choosing what meaning to take from selected Bible passages, then I think we could really hit it off. I speak very softly, so bring some kind of amplification device. I LOVE Back to the Future, because in it they go back to the '50s. It should be called that, really, shouldn't it? LOL. My dream would be to go there and stay there so if you have a time machine, drop me a line. LOL.
PS I know time machines don't exist. I'm not crazy! LOL! (I am. LOL.)

Username: SoundOut
Hobbies: Going to music festivals you haven't heard of yet, wearing no make-up in an obvious way, being really modest all the time. Walking.
Star sign: Patchwork
Just thought I'd give this a go. Sure, why not? My

*friends would describe me as sound, but it killed me
having to write that because it probably makes me
seem like a total big head. But they're making me write
this, so here goes. I'm sound (apparently – cringe) and
no one can understand why I'm single but I think
it's because I value people so much and I don't want
to risk friendships by getting involved. I'm looking
for someone who's sound. You don't have to be rich,
or anything, or even have a job, if you're passionate
about what you do, like writing one short film forever,
creating recycling sculptures, or knitting the truth.
I don't mind if you're male or female so long as you
have a beard. That probably makes me sound really
superficial – sorry! – I just really like beards. I'm in a
band called The Combovers: we cover French torch
singers using combs-and-paper and we got a great
review in* Hot Press. *I don't drink, I love cake and
I'm sound. If you're a sound, beardy, baker, and you
have a comb, let's make music together sometime.*

Username: Ee-i-ee-i-0
*I live on a farm so I don't meet a lot of people.
To be honest, I'm not gone on them, really. If you're
not threatened by strong business women who
enjoy the outdoors, give me a call. PS I'm a demon
in the hay.*

• • • • • ★ • • • • •

{ **COTTAGE INDUSTRY ALERT**: invent an
app called "Grandr". It's like Tinder or Grindr,
helping you locate other singles nearby who are
Grand. "It's how Grand people meet." }

• • • • ★ • • • • •

How To Marry an American

• • • • •

The pinnacle of every Irishwoman's achievement is to marry an American. St Brendan went ahead of Columbus to discover the Americas on the lookout for matches. That's how seriously he took it.

If other nationalities bought into the American Dream, we held onto it like a life-raft. If you had a family member Inamerica (all one word), they might send home letters with tales of wondrous things, like pizza, packaway raincoats, or money. Irish people thought that living Inamerica meant you lived on Easy Street – the O'Connell Street of most American towns.

Marrying an American meant you could live Inamerica now for as long as you liked. So here are the best ways to get one:

• • • • • ★ • • • • •

★ Go where there are Americans (e.g. Temple Bar, the Cliffs of Moher, the airport).

★ Be nice to Americans. Everyone's so mean to them these days, it disarms them.

★ Pretend you know how to date. Watch '80s films if you have to.

★ Be yourself but not really.

★ Watch the *Daily Show* and pretend you know the difference between Republicans and Democrats.

★ Say "Yes We Can" a lot.

★ Have a passport. This is exotic to them.

★ Learn to make their mother's speciality dish but never, ever actually make it. This will be seen as an attempt to usurp. Not wise.

★ Let yourself go a bit. American women tend to be beautifully groomed. Set yourself apart by offering them a bit of variety.

If we're honest, what you're really after is an Irish American. Someone who thinks that names like O'Gillahony are real – partly because that's their name. Someone who's never been to Ireland before, so you can lie about how bad things were for you growing up and get lots of sympathy. Someone who thinks you're a genius of co-ordination because you can drive

on the left. Americans tend to be open and trusting, so are the perfect balance to our jaded, cynical Irish heads.

But we are culturally different. Get this: when they ask someone to "make sure and look them up when they're in town", they mean it! Irish people invite all around them all over the world, and then get the shock of their lives when Brad actually arrives on the doorstep with his backpack. There follows a hurried re-enactment of the *Diary of Anne Frank* as various family members are hidden and lights switched off in an attempt to persuade Brad that you never existed. You have to change your number and move house. You should have just been honest, like Americans are. You should have said "I never want to see you again" while you were still in that noodle house in Thailand. That'll teach you.

My Big Fat Irish Wedding

So you've found yourself an American, or somehow bumped into another Irish person long and often enough that you've decided you want to keep bumping into each other periodically for the rest of your lives. Congratulations! Now you have to have an Irish Wedding.

Irish people love to party. We've so little faith that things will go our way, we toast every single thing that does. Even toast: if those two little feckers pop up not burnt, we call all our

friends and arrange a hoe down. At 8 in the morning.

Most Irish people can't believe they're even alive. We've had a lot of bad luck: it's a nice surprise if we wake up. Add a dark, cold climate and it's no wonder half of us have the blues on a semi-permanent basis. It makes for some great songs, but it's a tough old station and you'd need the odd break from it.

So, when something good happens, we pull out all the stops in an attempt not just to celebrate what's happened, but to prolong and share it. After all, if you're happy on your own, how will you know if you're happy when you fall in the woods? Do you make a happy sound? You need people there, to be sure.

Irish weddings are second only to funerals on our list of celebrations. They're some of the most glorious occurrences on the planet, but there are a lot of rules:

• • • • • ★ • • • • •

IRISH WEDDING RULES

1. Invite EVERYONE. You shouldn't know half of the people at it. It's not your day. It's theirs.
2. Turkey & ham. That's the menu. You can relax about that. Actually, if you wouldn't be averse to a turkey & ham cake, you should go ahead and have one. A grand bit of white sauce instead of icing. You'll make a lot of older Irish relatives very happy.
3. Dancing. Mercifully, the only time you will ever

see all age groups together on the dancefloor in Ireland is at a wedding. It doesn't matter what the music is, everyone's so happy that it's not a funeral, they'll be on their feet as soon as dinner's over.

4. The fourth rule of Irish weddings is: don't talk about Irish weddings. You will see things at them you will wish you could unsee. You will observe people performing acts upon cakes/other people that wouldn't be out of place in Ancient Rome. What happens at an Irish wedding stays at an Irish wedding.

5. If you're single, don't go. Yes, statistically it's not uncommon for couples to meet at weddings, but this is Ireland. Every distant relative will be trying to pair you up with somebody, asking repeatedly why "a lovely girl like you is still single". The first time you hear it, it's sweet. By the thirtieth time, you find yourself in tears and drunk dialling an unsuitable ex, e.g. the groom. Nobody expects the Irish Inquisition. Well, at a wedding, you should.

6. Ditto if you're newly married and not "yet" pregnant. You will be asked questions about yours and your partner's anatomies involving thicknesses and temperatures of things that even you're not sure of. Send a beautiful gift. But don't go.

7. A registry office wedding will do. But be

prepared for whispers of "Where's the priest?"
or "Is this it?", and hymns starting up from the
congregation whether you want them to or not.

8. Irish brides tend to be the thinnest women on
the island, and not in a good way. I suppose, as
we're already invisible a lot of the time, we have to
aim high. Or low, in kilo terms. And with so many
relatives squashed into one space, it probably makes
sense for the guest of honour to want to take up as
little of it as possible. But really, it's a terrible idea.
If nothing else will deter you from dieting, think
about this: you'll be freezing. You can't wear a
jumper on your wedding day.

9. Same-sex weddings are the best bits of the best
Irish weddings, with better music and dancing.
If you think you've waited your whole life for
someone, imagine the level of celebration if you've
only just got the right to do it? The marriage
equality referendum will be held in 2015 and it
just has to go through, for the weddings alone.

10. Irish weddings are huge, fun affairs. Don't even
try to have a quiet, low-key one. It might suit you
just grand, but again, this day is not about you.

Irotica: Grand Erotica

•••••

We all know how successful *Fifty Shades of Grey* was, and how terrible it was too. So what we've learned is that women like erotica and aren't afraid to read it on the bus. Progress. But it was *terrible*. It's great that a woman benefitted from the proceeds to the tune of millions of euro, but surely we can ask for more? Are pants hanging loosely from hips really the pinnacle of our fantasies?

Erotica should be good craic. After all, sex is, no matter what they say.

We haven't asked all of them individually, but Irish women surely have some of the best fantasies in the world. For so long we were told we could only imagine sex, but we weren't to. So of course, it was pretty much all we did.

We're so far past boring old whips and chains, surely *Fifty Shades* can't have done very well here? And if it did, it can only be because people thought it was an updated version of *Forty Shades of Green*, a lovely song about Irish grass: *Fifty Shades of Grey: a look at Modern Ireland, through a mist, with particular focus on the advent of cement.*

We feel there's room for a more Irish brand of erotica on the market. Here's some Grand Irish erotica (or Irotica).

• • • • • ★ • • • • •

GRAND IROTICA

Sheela tentatively approached the front door of the big house, a dozen hens' eggs pressed close to her ample bosom. The eggs were in a basket that swung by her side, but her bosoms were so ample that they were still bosom adjacent. Tentatively, on tip-toe, she rang the enormous door bell, and waited. It seemed like hours. Because it was. No one was home, and the smooth, firm eggs were cooling in the basket. "I should never have boiled them," thought Sheela, tentatively resting her bosom for a moment on the intricate cast-iron railing at the top of the steps.

Suddenly, a horse broke through the misty darkness. On it (the horse) was a handsome man. The kind of man who'd break an egg with just a look. Thank goodness she had hard-boiled them after all. It was dark, but Sheela could still tell the man was handsome. She could smell his handsomeness, circling like a sexy fog. Was it the tingling between her legs that brought her to this tantalising conclusion? Or the fact that he was closer now, and lit, because the horse had been moving while she was musing? Oh yes, he was handsome. And tall. Even off the horse, which he now was.

His jet black hair bristled in the moonlight as he strode towards her – which was a tad unnecessary; he was a good deal too close for striding – but something about this unnecessary striding made his thighs look firmer in the moonlight. Sheela was excited, albeit tentatively so. She gathered up her bosom, and curtsied.

"Who are you? And what are you doing at my 18th-century house?" bellowed the handsome man, breaking an egg with a look, even though it was hard-boiled.

"I have eggs," said Sheela.

The silence danced between them as she scrutinised his handsome face more closely, revealing even more handsomeness.

"You certainly have," he snarled kindly.

Was he looking at her bosom? Sheela couldn't be sure. She hoped so. Then he said:

"Come inside. It's raining."

"Is it? I hadn't noticed," replied Sheela.

For a moment, both of them were disappointed in her. But gathering up her bosom and eggs in a shawl she'd knitted for that very purpose, she would protest no longer. It was indeed raining. Handsome and capable of noticing weather, this man was dangerously attractive. As was being inside and dry. Or maybe wet …?

The horse reared up symbolically as the huge oak door creaked open, then disappeared across the lawn in a cloud of muck. The man led Sheela into a curiously lit hallway. Who had lit it? And how? And why? Sheela thought all these things with her mind as her body followed the man deeper into the house. He was even more handsome from the back, yet somehow more stern, if that were possible. Sheela loved this about him, and the tingle between her legs grew to a howl.

"You must be wet," said the man. "Let's get you out of those wet

things. You can't walk back to Ballyeggs House tonight."

"Indeed sir, that's where I live. But how did you …?" began Sheela, but the man laid a handsome finger on her lips, as if to say "Shut up, I'm the man." But he didn't say that.

He said, "I asked your mistress, Mrs Shellby, to send someone with the eggs. You must be new. They usually send an old crone."

"She's dead," whispered Sheela, with difficulty, for the man's finger was still on her lips.

The man nodded. "I'm glad," he said, before turning on his handsome heels and pouring her a pint of whiskey. The good kind. The kind from out of a bottle.

It was dawning on Sheela (for she was a biteen slow) that this was the master of the house, the famed Captain Legend, a retired English officer who'd had to retire because his handsomeness was too distracting on the battlefield. But where were the staff? And how did she get so lucky? Her stomach lurched with the excitement.

The whiskey was going to her head now, and the roar between her legs got drunk as well. She unwrapped the shawl from around her and let her bosoms fall to their natural position. Captain Legend was bewitched. "I thought all the beautiful girls had emigrated by now, or died," he said wistfully, which was very nice of an English officer to be.

"Me, beautiful? Feck off!" blushed Sheela, giving him a puck in the arm and spilling half the whiskey in her excitement. It went all over her full 18th-century-style skirt.

"Oh, no," she pondered, "I'll be in confession for a week now. Soiling a skirt and wasting whiskey is at least 30 Hail Marys." Then she remembered where she was, and confession became a distant, future memory.

"Come here," boomed Captain Legend, and he patted the empty chair beside him. It was only now that Sheela noticed the harp, and realised they were in the drawing room. She really shouldn't be here, so why did her lady-bits roar for her to stay?

"Do you play?" said the Captain, noticing her noticing the harp. He fingered some of the strings. He may as well have fingered Sheela, and before she knew it, her hands were on the harp, and she was singing 'Eileen Aroon' as suggestively as she could.

Captain Legend seemed overcome by the chemistry between them, too, and he squatted behind her, his expert fingers nimbly and deftly plucking whatever strings they wanted, glancing and dancing and brushing off her own hands as they harped. Together. It sounded terrible but there was no one there to hear, so no matter. As they reached their crescendo, Sheela felt something firm at her back: it was Captain Legend's left hand.

"Saints be praised; is he after playing all that with one hand?" thought Sheela, forgetting that, now they had ceased playing, his hands could be anywhere.

Without words, he guided her and her bosom out of her seat, and over to the chaise longue.

"I'm afraid the guest chambers have all been barricaded up for

secret reasons. If you're staying, you will have to lay here," whispered the Captain, tersely, as if something was tautening his firm buttocks.

Sheela couldn't help herself. She grabbed his decorated lapels and kissed him. Hard. Luckily, it was not her first kiss or she would really have made a mess of it. She'd been practising on half the boys in Ballyeggs village in case something better came along. This was something better, she felt sure of it, and it was definitely coming along. Hard. Hands undoing, legs quivering, the harp somehow playing itself, they went at it on the chaise longue. Hard. Til morning.

At daybreak, Captain Legend swallowed an egg without chewing it, or even removing its shell. "It's Sunday," he growled. "Shouldn't you be going to Mass?" "I would," said Sheela, "but I've too much to confess. Now go and get me a nice cup of tea, I've an awful hangover."

Tentatively, Captain Legend realised he was in love.

• • • • • ★ • • • • •

Look, it's just an idea, but it will probably be a bestseller. Please send your casting suggestions on a postcard. There will definitely be a terrible film.

8

YOU'RE
GRAND:
THE SECRETS
REVEALED

You now hold the key to living a Grand life – loads of keys, in fact, including the biggest, sexiest one of all. But there are even more less well-known secrets and we're about to share them with you now. With a few of these in your pocket, your life can be truly Grand. Maybe no more than Grand, but you know by now not to ask for more than that. It'll do.

A Note on Actual Secrets: The Secret Paradox

•••••

Irish women have had generations to get used to hiding people and holding clandestine meetings and not admitting things. So why can't we keep secrets? We're even about to spill the beans on some of our best ones here. But we like the look of you, and sure, you'd never tell. Would you?

A secret in Ireland is incredibly hard to define. We know what the word means in English, and we have a translation: rún, so we have heard of them. But our main problem with secrets is that they make excellent stories.

Don't belittle this secret-swapping by calling it "gossip" – this is the core of our society. Stories were our only entertainment, social interaction, currency. We may not have had food or a ticket out of here, so our consolation prize was knowing who else was coming or going and who they were coming or going with.

It's not that you can't trust us. You CAN. You can trust that your secret's safe with us as long as we don't bump into someone who'd really benefit from hearing it, or we need it to trade for information. Or a pint.

Anyway: here are extra Grand secrets for you. They may seem random, at first glance, but we promise they will change your life for the Grand-er. (Not to be confused with our new dating app: Grandr, although this may also change your life.)

Grand Products We Can't Live Without

· · · · · ·

For a real, Grand, Irishwoman, there are certain things you won't be able to go without for more than 24 hours. At the very least, you'll need to know they're within easy reach in a

nearby store-cupboard, should you need a fix. They're our anchors: without them we feel homesick, even if we haven't left the house. I'm not saying we're addicted to these things, but if deprived of or distanced from them for longer than a few days, we will get someone to smuggle them to us in a suitcase or write very sad songs about them.

Tayto Crisps

Chocolate in a purple wrapper

Irish butter. Deep, salty, yellow stuff

Rashers

Really salty soup

Atlantic sea salt

Ireland's Own

The Christmas *RTÉ Guide*

Dew

Election posters

Tea (your family's chosen brand)

Plastic bags – so good you have to pay for them

How To Piss an Irishwoman Off

• • • • • •

Whether you're an Irishwoman or you just know one, at certain crucial moments you will be faced with an opportunity to go over to the Dark Side. You have potential to use this next knowledge for evil. This would not be Grand. Try to use the following as a list of pitfalls to avoid rather than weapons to be used against us and you might just live to tell the tale. You do not want to unleash The Wrath:

THE WRATH:
AN IRISHWOMAN SCORNED

The Wrath of an Irishwoman is like a grenade wrapped in a volcano that's swallowed a keg of dynamite. We don't even need to have been scorned that badly for it to go off, you only need to have messed us about a little bit. If that happens, you will *wish* you'd been cursed from a height. If The Wrath were a film with yer man from *Nightmare on Elm Street* in it, he would not come out of it well.

Now, you'll notice that many of the following potential explosions are triggered by injustice – real or perceived, it doesn't matter. This time, it's personal.

★ Tell her she has to work the day of an All-Ireland final, or when the Ireland football squad has a match anywhere.

★ Tell her a neighbour won the Lotto. Especially if they're a bit of a nob.

★ Sing her party piece at a do, just before she gets up.

★ Bring her on a surprise romantic weekend … in Ireland. Nothing against the Shannon region, but she'll be keen to pack something sexier than wellies.

★ Offer her a coat if it rains when she's wearing a

dress, thereby questioning both her practical nature and her hardiness. Unforgivable. If she'd needed a coat, she'd have brought one, thank you very much. And she doesn't need a coat. She has a jumper.

★ Take her to a raw restaurant. Irish people in general think these are makey-uppy.

★ Refer to her as a mucker or a bogger. Even if she is, it's for her to say, not you.

★ Neglect to tell her she has "a lovely colour" when she comes back from Spain.

★ Agree when she bitches about her family. Do not even go near this one.

★ Tell her she can't do something. Anything. Then run.

How To Fake Mass

• • • • •

At some point, you'll have to go to Mass. No matter how much Ireland has changed recently, Catholicism and its rituals are still at the heart of lots of important events. Even if you're not a believer, many of your friends will be and you can't not show up to their inevitable funerals.

There are many wonderful practising Catholics in Ireland today. They are amazing, because loads of them can actually sit through a whole Mass. Even a jazzed-up Mass with cool guitar

players and priests mentioning *Downton Abbey* in the sermon. Actually, especially those.

In recent years, Ireland has seen a massive increase in religious diversity, and many lapsed Catholics have stopped going to Mass: that's a lot of people who have forgotten the moves, if they ever knew them in the first place. Up? Down? Kneel? Who can say? What to do if you have to go to a wedding in a Catholic setting? It's potential chaos.

Well, fear not: here's How to Fake Mass.

★ So, you've decided to go to Mass. Well done. You're probably missing out on a match or some craic but there'll be plenty of craic in Heaven when the "cool kids" are roasting "down below".

★ So how does Mass go? Listen, you will <u>never</u> get all the words and moves right. No one ever has. Besides, they keep switching them up to keep things fresh and catch out heathens. So be a bit behind. Copy everyone else. Kneel when they kneel, bow when they bow, genuflect whenever in doubt.

★ Every now and again, throw in a move of your own – a hand movement here, a chest-thump there – to mix things up a little. Nothing too showy, you don't want to be disrespectful: just a half-turn or a cheeky side-bend. You'll be amazed at how many people join in. Loads of people don't really know

how Mass goes. You are not alone.

★ The Sign of Peace takes many newcomers by surprise. In many countries, they say "Peace be with you" and embrace. NOT HERE. Shake hands. Do not linger or smile or make too much eye contact. You don't want to ruin everything. This is MASS.

★ Treat holy water like a fine cologne. It's considered de rigueur to use a little, but using too much is crass. Keep it classy. Keep it Massy.

$$\cdots \star \cdots$$

SKIPPING MASS: MASSION IMPOSSIBLE

Being a heathen is one thing. No one really cares if you go to Mass because you're a lost cause anyway. But what if you want to score brownie points with, say, a super-devout iMOM-in-law?

Skipping Mass or leaving early is very risky and I don't recommend it. If you're supposed to be there, BE THERE. It's just less stressful. You might be seen leaving. You might be asked what the sermon was, and what you thought of the cool new priest's analogies. If you missed both Mass *and Downton Abbey*, you really are in trouble. How to pull it off?

1. Go to the start of Mass. Be seen praying. Be heard praying, or at least mumbling something indistinct at the right moments. Then slip out while the priest creates a distraction with the miracle of transubstantiation. The very devout won't notice. If they do, they'll have to admit to not praying hard enough. You have them there.

2. Take the Mass leaflet with you. Make up what the sermon might have been. Throw in something about *Downton*, or how life is like a golf course, and you probably won't be far off. If you're playing the long game, it's worth finding out the priest's interests and hobbies.

3. WARNING: Some iMOMs know the sermons by heart. Not just from one Mass, all of them. Unless you bribe an altar boy for intel, you might as well forget it. You're trapped. Ask a teenager to smuggle you out. They are expert Mass leavers. No one can burrow you out of Mass quicker than a 17 year old.

How To Confess

•••••

If you're going to do Mass, technically you should go to confession first. It's not like you haven't been sinning: you're a woman, after all.

You probably haven't been to confession for months, maybe years. And right off the bat, you're meant to 'fess up (literally) to when you were last there. You do not want to waste valuable absolution time on discussion of your social calendar. Even the youngest Irish girl knows the following trick for when that grille goes back next time you're in the confessional:

"Bless me, Father, for I have sinned. It has been ... a ... while ... since my last confession."
"A while? How long, my child?"
Long silence. He cracks his knuckles.
"How long, my child?"
"Thr — No, two weeks. It has been two weeks since my last confession."

Your voice will have trembled here, because this is NOT TRUE, but STICK TO THE PLAN.

Very good, my child. But you know it's very bad to miss confession? Even the one week."
"Yes, Father."
"And you'll be here every week from now on?"
"Yes, Father." *Not a chance.*
"Very good. Now, tell me your sins."
"Well, I lied, Father. To a priest."

"Oh dear, well that is very bad. Ten Hail Marys, 44 Our Fathers, now get out of my box."

And there you have it. Your get-into-Mass-free card. It works, but you shouldn't feel particularly proud of yourself.

······ ★ ······

How To Make a Grand Bit o' Brown Bread

·····

This recipe is from genius brown soda bread maker Mary Flynn, who's allowing us to share it with you here. Serving brown bread you've baked yourself will up your Grand quotient no end.

Mary Flynn can't stress enough that these measurements are approximate, and – like all good things Irish women can do – you can only really discover what you like and what works with practice.

The measurements are in Imperial because that's the way of things. If you want other measurements use a converter, like the American cousins, or move to France.

INGREDIENTS:

Semolina, to dust baking tin ("The very best for non-sticking": Mary Flynn)

1 level tsp Turmeric

1 level tsp Salt

1 heaped tsp Bread Soda.

8 oz Wholemeal Flour

2 oz Polenta

2 oz Coarse Bran

2 oz Wheat Germ

2 oz Sesame Seeds (toast these and the wheat germ in oven if you feel like showing off)

1 not too huge tbsp Molasses (more if you like your bread dark. Or if you love molasses)

2 tbsps Rapeseed Oil (or other)

12 fl. oz Buttermilk or Soya Milk (if using soya, "sour up" with 1 tbsp vinegar or lemon juice)

FOR STARTERS

- Oil a 1lb loaf tin and dust it well with semolina.
- Next turn oven on to 220°C or 425°F: you will need it fully heated so you can put mixture straight in to bake once wet and dry ingredients have been combined. No messing.
- For mixing, you'll need a fork and a perforated plastic spoon, or your hands. You know you want to.

If substituting soya milk, "sour up" with vinegar for 5 to 15 mins. You can do this in advance and keep it in the fridge. (Put it in a glass and children will love watching it change.) Don't use until sour, or the bread soda won't react and rise (and the bread will have that horrible metallic taste sometimes found in Irish soda bread. But not on Mary Flynn's watch).

NEXT UP

- Put all the small ingredients into the bowl first. Press any lumps out of the bread soda lumps (vital) and mix.
- Use perforated spoon or your womanly hands to gradually add rest of dry ingredients, lifting to incorporate air. Hum if you like (can't hurt).
- Warm a little of the milk to soften molasses.
- Add oil to rest of milk.
- Make a hollow in dry ingredients and pour liquids in. Now, lightly, with fork, draw everything together from outside in. Mixture should be damp and a little loose: not completely stuck together.

IT'S TIME TO TAKE IT TO THE TIN ...

- Spoon mixture into tin, making a bit of contact with sides. Fork it down into place but don't press too much. If you squash it in, it will be very tough.
- Cover lightly with tinfoil.

- No messing: put straight into fully heated oven and test after half an hour. Stick in a skewer: bread is done when it comes out "clean". If not fully cooked, leave a little longer.
- If semolina is used for greasing tin, bread can be removed fairly soon. "Knock" on the base: if it sounds hollow, you're done.
- Cool on a wire rack and don't cut until cold. (This is nonsense. Mary never did this. You want stuff to melt on it.)
- Serve. Be careful of the compliments you get on how Grand all this makes you seem. You don't want to think you're great, no matter how good your bread is.

How To Write a Grand Poem

•••••

All Irish people are poets. Hardly any of us are good poets, but that doesn't stop us writing poems all the time.

Loads of young Irish women are good at maths and science and are excelling at them on the global stage (although someone should tell them it won't help at their interview to be an iMOM of the Skies. They should be focussing on fry-cooking and perfecting one phrase in Irish). But whatever your own natural strengths, we are all encouraged to be good at words, so we can

all have a go at poems too! It's the land of (male) saints and (male) scholars, but even girls can have a go. All you need is a quill and some vellum, or a stone and some kind of scrawling implement and away for road with you.

Songs are great, everyone loves them; and what are songs only poems put to music? The difference with poems is that – even if you're not musical – you won't be left out. No wordsmith left behind.

You're probably itching to get scribbling right now, but first a few pointers. There are thousands of years of wisdom in here, so you might want to make yourself a pot of tea first. Here's what should go into a Grand Irish poem:

● ● ● ● ● ★ ● ● ● ● ●

★ Loss. Always loss. You've lost something or someone and you're not best pleased.

★ Never seeing the likes of something again.

★ Having never said a good word about Ireland in your life, you're currently in exile somehow and nothing will do you but to get back there as quickly as possible.

★ The land. The land must feature in the form of cliffs, glens, mountains. Even better: stones or soil or stony grey soil.

★ The sea. Preferably rolling between you and something.

★ Names. Lovers (first names only) or enemies (surnames only).

★ Have you made sure to put in some loss?

★ Prison. Can be literal or metaphorical, but you're in some kind of jail or, better yet, *gaol*.

★ A broken heart. Or a scalded one. Basically, something's up with the old ticker.

Bonus points for name-checking a crop of some kind. Extra points again if it's failed.

★ A horse.

★ Great mythological heroes straddling stuff.

★ Thighs (firm = hero; quivering = sex).

★ Bogs.

★ Questionable rhyming scheme.

★ Something about England.

★ More loss.

And here's an example of how that all might come together:

IRELAND POEM

Your loss hangs heavy upon my exiled shoulders as
I scan the people-sodden beach at Tenerife
Compounding – oh – my grief

TARA FLYNN

That I will never see your likes again – not for some days
A clifftop shout brings nothing back but air breathed
into hollow lungs
That gasp to breathe you in
The soil is dry and parched
Like Harrington's heart, and the cottages torched
I long for stones beneath my feet and muck to squelch
between my beachy toes and broken heart
Scalded from the lack of you, dear Ireland
A great sea rolls between us, unlike the muck that
isn't there
Island calls to island, arms outstretched, sunburnt
and empty
My thighs are sunburnt too, like Fionn MacCumhaill,
He would have straddled this great distance in one step
had he the sunblock
They say the corn is coming in. I hope it won't go
out again.
Horse passes bog, manless – both horse and bog
And bog oak whispers "Deirdre: I could be a tree were
I not bogged"
My grief, my loss, my sunburn catalogued:
I miss my mammy's dhinners

Don't let us see you back here until you've won some kind of prize for literature.

How To Sing

•••••

In the last section we said that poems were great if you weren't musical. We lied! Of course you're musical. You're Irish, and we'll be damned if you're going to miss out on one of the most popular clichés about us. Of all the clichés we might as well accept about ourselves, singing is one of the good ones.

The tell-tale sign of an evening having been A Great Night (much, much better than a Grand one) is whether it ends up with everyone singing. In unison or with solos of varying degrees of skill, after a certain point, someone will ask the host to turn off the music or shut the shop or postpone the open-heart surgery so everyone can have a sing.

It's easy. I promise.

1. Clear your throat.
2. Close your eyes.
3. Open your mouth and let it out with gusto. The quality of the noise coming out isn't important, it's the gusto you're after.
4. Cry when someone else is singing; partly because you're moved at the great beauty of their vocal prowess, partly because you're sad it's not your turn.

5. NB: Make them work for your turn. Don't be a pushover. You may be bursting but spend about an hour insisting you won't do a song, then give in and do ten. It's important to get them to pester you so you can then outstay your welcome in revenge.

6. Bring an annoying instrument wherever you go. The more people groan when they see you coming with it, the better the instrument.

7. Comment loudly all the way through others' songs: "Good man yourself!" "Yes!" "Beautiful!" If you can do any of this in Irish, so much the better.

8. When you're done singing, you get a Noble Call, which means you can nominate who sings next. Make sure it's the most reluctant singer in the room. This is a sing-song. Discomfort is part of the craic.

9. Applause isn't enough. Whoop, cheer, break things. These people have been forced to sing against their will, and you've all had to suffer the consequences. It's time for yet more good old cathartic release.

10. Spend all your time between now and the next "session" learning at least 3 new songs. It doesn't matter if they're shite. They just have to be ready.

How To Be Grand in Television Interviews

•••••

As has already been pointed out, pretty much every Irishwoman will end up on TV at some point, so we'd better have a look at what you're going to be asked in an interview. Preparation is everything.

A quick way to take the temperature of a country with regard to women is to see how interviewers deal with them. On the national broadcaster, or in the press, what kind of questions are they asking? Are they holding "personality" competitions involving "closed-door bikini contests"?

There aren't a ton of Irish women on the airwaves just yet. There are some great female journalists, current affairs minds and askers of questions working to change things, but for now it's best to assume that when you go on TV or radio your interviewer will be male.

Unless the interviewee is also a straight white male, many Irish interviewers get their Y-fronts in a bit of a twist. But we have to be gentle with them; they're not women: how can they possibly be expected to know what to ask us, let alone where to look? Sure, they've no idea what goes on in women's heads at all, poor fellas.

Tip 1. Go easy on them. They've been indoctrinated for years and years with the idea that women will be the ruin of them. No wonder they're uneasy when we pop up on a live broadcast with our breasts ahead of us.

Tip 2. If they ask "What does hubby do?" don't get offended. It's not their fault. The "Questomatic 500", a rusty old question generator kept in a basement, is too expensive to update. And if a question appears on their list THEY HAVE TO ASK IT. Or they will be killed.* (*Taken off TV.)

Tip 3. Wear knee-pads. You will be patted on the knee and some of those guys are big. Hopefully, there'll be a desk in the way and you'll be alright unless he has very long arms.

Tip 4. Don't pat his knee back. That would be "suggestive" or "inappropriate" coming from you. You don't want to make a fool of yourself.

Tip 5. You will definitely be asked about the home–life balance: how do you make movies/write books/discover cures for contagious diseases and still make sure the home runs smoothly? Just say you freeze a lot of stuff in advance.

Tip 6. Dress well, but not too sexily, i.e. revealing any flesh at all. Wear something in a nice tweed, with plenty of scarves. You'll be promoting Irish industry, and not putting the interviewer in the compromising position of being unable to control himself. Your goal, as ever, should be to put him at ease.

Tip 7. If you have kids, start every answer with "As a mother". Especially if there's an argument to be won. Irish men would never argue with their mothers or anyone else's.

Tip 8. If you don't have kids, you will 100% be asked when you are having them. Not if. Say soon, or next Tuesday, or start to cry … anything but "I'm not planning a family". This is most likely a family show and no place for freaks. Just say you freeze a lot of stuff in advance. Namely eggs.

Tip 9. Relax, but not too much. Men on TV are allowed to relax, spread out and sit with their crotch on full view to the world. Not you, though, even in jeans. So, knees together, crotch tucked in. Take up as little space as possible. Know your place.

Tip 10. Don't say what you really mean about complex topics such as equality. It might just be a bit too much for the poor lad to process, and he won't be sure whether to agree or not without checking with someone. You don't want an interviewer to have a coronary live on air, no matter how hard you want to push your new single. Say you're Grand. Because you are.

Keep smiling! No one likes a strident woman to react adversely to being patronised on national TV!

And you're all set. When you get that call to go on TV, you'll be ready. But just in case you are actually happier being a bit more peripheral to the limelight, or you don't have knee pads …

How To Be Everybody in the Audience

•••••

The healing of the long old rift between Ireland and Britain continues, sometimes in ways you wouldn't expect. Like when the Queen of England came over, made a significant bow, and was pictured smiling at a market in Cork.

So excited was the Queen by this whole smiley adventure that she invited the President back over to her gaff: she gave over the entire Royal Albert Hall to *Céiliúradh* – a night of Irish music, poetry and song. U2 weren't at it, but it seemed to go off OK.

Here, in the most English of settings, were people from both countries whooping and cheering and generally getting down. So much so that they got comfortable enough to reveal themselves to be what we'd suspected all along: an Irish Audience.

The natural habitat for the Irish Audience is a television studio in a full state of ready-to-wave-at-the-camera arousal. You might even catch a few of them wandering around the back of The News, hands at the ready. Here's how to recognise an Irish Audience:

★ waving at the camera

★ nudging each other and grinning as if you've never seen a camera before

★ easily startled by a moving or controversial item, such as mention of the word "condom"

★ checking under your seats for free stuff, such as a weekend away or a knitting pattern

★ wearing your absolute best, even better than you'd wear for Mass or to grease up an American for souvenir money

★ saying hello to your iMOM, even if she's beside you in the studio

★ THE BIGGIE: When music comes on, CLAP ALONG. OUT OF TIME

As an Irish Audience member, it's all about joining in. It's primal, it's shared; as unifying as the muck beneath our feet. Being part of an Irish Audience transcends the present moment and hooks you up to the full Irish matrix. It's about as Irish as you can be.

When they all clapped in the Albert Hall, it was very moving. It was also proof of something we'd long suspected: you can take the clapping-along-out-of-time audience out of Ireland, but you can't take Ireland out of the clapping-along-out-of-time audience.

What a Waste
•••••

Ireland's always in, just coming out of, or about to enter a recession. If not a recession, you can be sure some other kind of disaster would be about to befall us. We just have no luck! Of course, we're Grand, but we always have to be on our toes, and we can't take a single thing for granted. That's why Irish women try not to throw out anything that might someday come in useful. We can't abide waste.

Here are some of the things Irish women consider a bit of a waste:

★ Any leftover food that hasn't grown legs and walked out by itself. Couldn't you put it in a soup? Bringing it to the boil gets rid of any unsavoury unidentifiable bits

★ Leaving the immersion on any longer than you need

★ Reboiling the kettle. You should know "a cup (of tea)" measure by weight. One boil only

★ Running the tap. Are you sure you're thirsty?

★ Cast offs. If you don't want it, we'll have it

★ Watching the Eurovision sober

★ Vegetarianism

★ Air conditioning

★ Handsome priests

A Grand Vest

•••••

In the spirit of not wanting to waste anything, you don't want to let any bit of heat escape, especially through your jumper. When we were warrior queens we had armour, and did a lot more running around.

Now, we have vests. Vests aren't just for children with asthma, oh no. They work alongside being a Grand Hoult to keep us safe and warm. Invisible, like a super power, your granny would never have let you leave the house without your vest, so neither will we.

Have you your vest on? Oh, it might have sleeves now, or be disguised as a t-shirt with thermal properties. You might even be calling it "layering", but every Irishwoman knows that the vest is the source of much of her power.

1. It's why the scratchiest of jumpers never irritates our skin.

2. It's another reason why we don't get cold.

3. It creates a nice seam-free line over more elaborate lingerie.

4. It helps insults to bounce right off.

5. If tea is a cure, then the vest is a vaccine, warding off everything from TB to kidney failure to something about evil spirits. Yer Gran said so.

Invest in a vest, your chest will thank you.

Grand Superheroines

• • • • •

Now you know part of the source of our everyday powers, there's no avoiding this fact: we need more Irish Superheroines. We've come up with some suggestions. Get started, animators.

THE GREEN WIDOW

This woman used to be a spy. There's nothing she doesn't know about the people on her road. She will share this intel only in the strictest confidence with her closest allies (Bridie from No. 6) or if she's drunk. A keen kitchen gardener, she was a very loyal wife til her husband died trying to get her an extremely rare shrub from the edge of a cliff. So rare that the shock of coming across it brought on a heart attack, although everyone assumed that he fell. The Green Widow has never forgiven herself, and to this day she can't even look at a hill – in fact, she doesn't even really like to go upstairs anymore. Heights are her kryptonite. Just as well her superpowers are listening and peering, which can be done on the down low. Literally. She got her name when she refused to wear black to the funeral, swathing herself instead in the leaves she and her husband loved in happier times.

BATMAMMY

Batmammy works in the local church, cleaning and making sure everything is neat and super-holy. She looks after everyone – especially Father Danger, the daredevil priest – and spends a lot of time in the belfry, hence her name. There is a suspicion that something is going on between her and Father Danger, but others say that she keeps him close in order to foil any evil plans he might cook up. After all, he has a motorbike and that can't be his real name. Batmammy can only foil crimes that happen in or near the church: she sees a lot from her belfry, but by the time she gets down all the steps the crook has usually got away, and she's been too far off to be a reliable witness. She once foiled a mugging in the graveyard, by tripping the mugger up with a broom as he tried to escape. She has a utility belt in which she carries a screwdriver, a feather duster, loads of chammies and a bottle of Brasso that never runs out. Batmammy has been heard to mutter that if only she could polish crime away, this town would be a lot shinier.

THE SWIRLING MIST

This mysterious woman seems to be everywhere, even on the driest of days. But it's an illusion. Swirling Mist ("Swirls" to her friends) is the only one of our heroines who's a scientist herself. Originally American, she fell in love with Ireland while looking for gold at the end of the rainbow. So obsessed did she become

with this quest, that she set up a lab down the country experimenting on the effects of precipitation on gold and tiny shoes. One such experiment went horribly wrong, and she herself was cast into a million droplets, becoming the mist that makes up the rainbow itself. It is a terrible superpower: although it enables her to eavesdrop on discussions about the location of treasure, her presence is given away by obvious damp patches. Needless to say, she has never married. Although she did manage to meet tiny arch villain The Leprechaun once, when he came to her lab, and there was no doubt that they had chemistry.

THE COTTAGE

The Cottage refers to a collective of women who work in folk parks by day. They make brown bread, they weave, they smudge fake dirt on themselves and are really sad about the Famine for the tourists. But by night, they're a crack team of kick-boxing, abseiling, special force branch cops. They realised in the late '70s that tourists let their guard down in Ireland because they think we're all eejits. Just by weaving away quietly in the background, they overhear all kinds of crimes being planned as arch villains fit in a bit of plotting, while tracing their Irish roots. Their most famous bust was of an Eastern European drug ring: Sheila overheard them plotting in Russian over by the fully-functional spinning wheel. At closing time, she and the other Cottagers slipped into their combat gear and took the

secret tunnel behind the giant fully-functional fireplace, leading to one of the fanciest hotels in the land. (Criminals don't use B&Bs because B&Bs don't usually have brandy glasses they can swirl while plotting on the phone.) The crims were trussed up and handed over to Interpol before you could say *"Céad Míle Fáilte"*. Saoirse still had flour on her hands at the time.

ARAN WOMAN

Every Irishwoman has a jumper, we know that. But none is as attached to or as renowned for hers as Aran Woman. Like a woolly, female Iron Man, anytime trouble is near, Aran Woman slips into her armour: an oversized cardigan with big brown buttons. It was made in a knitting lab by the finest woolly minds available. Aran Woman (real name Mary Jumper) is the only depressed millionaire of the superheroines, and the only Protestant. She doesn't have any powers herself, she has to rely on the cardie. In times of crisis, without hesitation Mary jumps into the cardie, buttons it all the way to the top, and looks in a mirror. This doesn't actually foil anything, but Mary gets so absorbed in the intricate patterns that she's the only person around unbothered by crime, or even by a bit of bad news. Her Zen-like indifference has made her a heroine. Some people say it's denial, but we know the truth. She literally pulls the wool over her own eyes. Mary is currently a close adviser to the Taoiseach.

The Christmas

•••••

The Christmas is very important in Ireland for obvious religious and cultural reasons. But more than that, there's a reversal of the flow of the constant haemorrhaging of young people from the country. Everyone comes home. City mice become culchie mice again for a few days.

Over The Christmas, Irish women get a reminder of where they really come from. Midnight Mass is a great chance to see how everyone you knew at school has aged. There's a lot of pressure to look good and it's probably best to get in training around mid-November. But nobody does that, so it's all the one. Your best hope is that to their equally ageing, blurry peepers, you look exactly like you did last year. Blurry.

There is no Christmas Family Fight like an Irish Christmas Family Fight. People dig up insults so old they should get honorary archaeology degrees. If the Big Day ends without at least one family relationship irreparably damaged, then you've done The Christmas wrong. But it's somehow all put aside (if not forgotten) by the time the turkey sandwiches come out on Stephen's Day.

••••• ★ •••••

December 26th is St Stephen's Day, known in
Ireland as Stephen's Day. Or Stephen'ses Day. NOT

Boxing Day. I've no idea whether Stevo is a fake saint or not, but call "Stephen's Day" "Boxing Day" like our friend the Irish Roots Denier and you might just get a box.

● ● ● ● ● ★ ● ● ● ● ●

It's assumed that you go home to your family for The Christmas. It is the Irish way. If you want a fright, just try doing something different over The Christmas. We dare you. Try announcing it over the phone, to your iMOM. Hear that? Yes, that's the sound of the deafening silence of disappointment.

Here's a checklist for a Grand Irish (The) Christmas:

★ Ticket home. Book it in July at the latest. It will cost around €1,000,000. You will never find it harder to get into Ireland, or down the country.

★ Your walking shoes. You will need to get out of the house. A lot.

★ Sunglasses. Every light and candle in the house will be on.

★ A "hilarious" Christmas jumper. No one wants to feel left out at Christmas. You'll already be being treated as if you're your 16-year-old self, so you may as well up the self-loathing ante too.

★ Bigger trousers.

★ A highlighter pen. If you want to watch the

things you want to watch, you will have to highlight them in the *RTÉ Guide* before anyone else does. Beware: decoy *Guides* may have been bought by devious family members. Try and find the Original *RTÉ Guide* or you'll have to watch *Gladiator* again, as well as ALL the carol services from everywhere, along with anything Mary Kennedy is hosting.

★ Presents. For everyone. Even if they say they don't want anything because there's a recession on. You're not falling for that one again.

•••••★•••••

WOMEN'S CHRISTMAS/ LITTLE CHRISTMAS

We nearly forgot! Irish women have our very own Christmas! It's the 6th of January, and to celebrate Women's Christmas or Little Christmas (we're so feckin' *cute*), traditionally the men cook. That's right: we have a day for that. So have a day off, ladies! Kick back and watch *Rocky IV* or whatever is on, because even God wants you to relax today. She's probably having a day off today, too, after all the birthday hoo-ha round hers. At least it's an acknowledgement by Irish tradition of the work that has gone on over The (Real) Christmas, that turkeys don't just magically appear cooked and stuffed, with five different kinds of potato.

A realisation of some kind. What's the word again? Oh, yes: Epiphany.

• • • • • ★ • • • • •

St Patrick's Day

• • • • •

How to be an Irishwoman on St Patrick's Day.

• • • • • ★ • • • • •

ST PATRICK'S DAY IN IRELAND

1. Ignore the whole thing. You're proud to be Irish all year round, you don't need a day.
2. Complain loudly "It's more of a face-paint, tourist-trap, drinking festival now, isn't it?" at least once an hour.
3. Decide you absolutely, definitely need something only available in the centre of town, where the parade is. Seethe.
4. It's important to be really grumpy the whole day, or at least til about 5 o'clock. Then head to

your nearest pub, dressed head-to-toe in anything but emerald.

5. Gently rugby tackle anyone who mentions "St Patty" to the ground.

6. Lent: Even practising Catholics get St Patrick's Day off. If only poor Jesus had known that; a bit of chocolate on March 17th might have helped the rest of the days in the desert fly by. Anyway, even if you haven't been doing Lent, go mad on something, just 'cause. Ice cream. Whatever. So long as it's not green: that's for tourists.

ST PATRICK'S DAY ABROAD

1. This is your moment. Get up early so you can work it for all it's worth.

2. Tell everyone you're Irish.

3. Ramp up your accent. Say "begorrah" a lot. It'll make you die a little inside but it will most likely result in free food or drink.

4. Wear green or they will pinch you. It hurts. No one who lives in Ireland does this, so no, we don't know why either. But they do it, so you've been warned. Wear green, and your best look of disdain.

5. Did you mention that you're Irish?

6. Insist on everyone giving you a bite of their (green)

cookies or buying you a (green) beer. Bring a sick bag (any colour) with you everywhere, just in case.

7. Do not walk anywhere: insist on a sedan chair.

8. Remind everyone that you're Irish.

9. Relish it. For the rest of the year, we're ridiculed as fighting drinkers who've only ever produced one good band. On St Paddy's Day, we're the queens of the world.

10. Go to bed in your greenest jammies, secure that there'll be far fewer pinching incidents tomorrow. Or if there are, it'll be back to its rightful name of common assault.

•••••★•••••

Not Remembering Names
•••••

You're nearly ready to go out into the world, and mix with people as a Grand Irishwoman. New people, even. So you need to know this: Irish people are terrible at remembering names. That's why, as we've seen in Peig's day, everyone seems to have been called Cáit (or in America, Colleen). You had too much else to remember with all the dying and emigrating; names were just the last straw.

We've a lot more time for remembering now, and phones with memories in case ours fail. But even so, names still get

away from us. With all that pressure to seem lovely and friendly, forgetting someone's name really isn't on.

So, if you find yourself in a situation where you know the face but not the name, take these steps:

- ★ Act even friendlier.
- ★ Dazzle them with a beaming smile: even if they realise what you're up to, the brightness might make them forget.
- ★ Pat them on the back. Grab their arm a lot: anyone this tactile must remember your name; they're obviously just choosing not to use it.
- ★ Buy them a drink. For God's sake, buy them a drink.
- ★ Keep buying drinks until you either remember their name or they forget their own.
- ★ Pick a new name for them. Cáit, maybe. Use it loudly and often, ignoring them when they correct you. Soon, that's what everyone will call them and they'll have no choice but to change it by deed poll.

We know you thought we were great with names. We're not. And the more effusive we are with our handshakes and exclamations of "is it yourself?!", the less of a clue do we have as to what you're actually called. Sorry, tourists.

Grand Comfort in Discomfort

•••••

We're nearing the end of the book, and you're now about as Grand as can be expected – as Grand as anyone could hope to be – so we should probably cut to the chase. You want the truth? Can you handle it? Right, so.

Irish women don't actually really like misery. We're not that comfortable with it. It's grand, but of course we'd really prefer not to be miserable. It's more that we're not used to the absence of misery, so we're not quite sure where to look when it goes away. If our heart rates settle and our blood pressure drops, we wander around in a state of perpetual readiness, wondering what shite's going to drop on our heads next. The next miserable surprise can only be just around the corner!

Don't mistake this for pessimism. It's not. If Irish women were pessimistic there'd never be any festivals. But being braced for misery means that it can never quite get the drop on us. We're one step ahead.

And so, despite being perfectly Grand, it's important that Irish women stay a tiny bit uncomfortable at all times. Like misery ninjas: awake, prepared, suspicious. Put it this way: if Troy had been in Ireland, there's no way that horse would have got in.

So don't be surprised if, when you offer an Irishwoman a seat, she doesn't take it. It's not personal. It's just that the comfort

would wrong-foot her. But make sure you offer it, all the same. Otherwise, that next miserable surprise might just be for you.

Irish Women Don't Get Old

•••••

Irish women are born old already, so that's that done. We carry the weight of generations of misery (and constantly being braced for the next round of it) upon us; as we grow we learn all about the injustice *du jour*, and why we're probably to blame for it. Inequality deepens fine lines around the eyes and elsewhere. But we balance this misery with the craic; the craic keeps you feeling young, no doubt about it.

Middle age is probably the hardest time for an Irishwoman – no longer dewy-young and comely, but not yet Peig: getting through shite by not giving a feck takes training. Yet somehow our bodies seem to Hibernomorph from spring chicken to Peig almost overnight. That can be a shock if you're not prepared.

There's a major upside, however: in terms of giving less and less of a feck, Irish women age backwards. Eventually we're 80 and gleefully butting everyone who annoys us in the supermarket out of the way with a trolley, with all the joy of a kid on a swingset. There may be physical challenges as we revert to our inherited shape, but in many ways, these are our best years.

····· ★ ·····

HOW TO BE AN OLD IRISHWOMAN

★ Tell all the stories you've been stockpiling. You are now in the Peig Phase and will be perceived as very very wise indeed. Add a smokey cackle for even more depth.

★ Many women start to feel invisible as they age. Not old Irish women. We've been invisible for years. We know how to use it to our advantage.

★ Get a stick, in case you aren't in a supermarket when you come across annoying people and there isn't a trolley to hand. Just put on a cross old lady face and shake the stick.

★ Don't worry about creams: we simply haven't had enough sunlight to do much UV damage. Cloud cover is better than any anti-ageing cream. It's free and – finally! – a useful application for misery.*

*wear sunblock. This is a joke.

★ If you're being bothered by teenagers, start to tell them in graphic detail how you lost your virginity. They won't be long clearing off.

★ Keep Joe Duffy on speed dial. If you even think a thing, make sure the nation hears it on the radio. Do not keep any thought you have to yourself.

★ Use the free travel to take outings on the bus.

Dress up. Go with pals. Talk to everyone.

★ Having spent most of your life obsessed with death, the end isn't as difficult for the Irish. You've spent most of your life in shock that you're still around. When it's your time, you just hope for 2 things. 1. A good death and 2. that it should happen in Ireland. Now, we don't know what a good death is, really. We've never seen any reviews. But this is something old ladies say a lot – along with "She went very quickly in the end" about someone who's been going for at least a year. You may not want to die in Ireland. But for goodness' sake *say* that you do.

★ Plan your funeral with all the pep of a young bride. Think about any songs or flowers or video messages you might like, as well as whose people you'd actually like to be buried with. Then talk about these plans incessantly with your family, the top deck of the bus, or Joe. Obvs.

●●●●●★●●●●●

The best thing about being an old Irishwoman is that boldness, like a fine wine, also matures with age. We get so much bolder as we get older. So that's something to look forward to.

A Grand Day in the Life

•••••

Now you're completely immersed in Grand wisdom, and you're almost ready to just get out there and live it. But you shouldn't attempt it without a bit of a template: you wouldn't knit a jumper without a pattern, would you?

This is what your days should look like:

Dawnish: Wake. Remember you're raging about something. Have a grand cup of tay.

Just post-dawn: Make breakfast for husband and children: even if you don't have a husband and children. It's good practice for when you will. Slot in your beauty routine (dew, etc.) where possible.

9am: Go to work, raging. This can be in the house or out of it, but make sure toil is involved.

9.01am: Grand cup of tay. Chat.

10.17am: Resume toiling.

10.45am: Talk about the weather to colleagues/ neighbours. Make sure to leave time for whatever it is you're raging about.

11am: More tay.

1pm: The bit o' dhinner. Or, if you're less traditional, approx. 7 bites of a sandwich.

2pm: More toiling and tay. Maybe Talk to Joe if

you're *really* raging.

5.30pm: After toiling, try and fit in a walk, or a bit of protest marching. So many Irish women are raging, there's bound to be one near you.

7pm: Make and eat the tay (or bit o' dhinner, if you're modern or European). If you don't have a family, imagine that you have. Set the table for at least eight.

9pm: Watch something on TV, or go to the pub, making sure to include some time to be raging.

Later: Before bed, take in at least one current affairs programme to stir your already simmering rage.

Bedtime: *Oíche mhaith agus codladh sámh*. Raging.

What Irish Women Want

Everyone in the world wants to know: what is it Irish women want? It's something we've been wondering ourselves for years. Well, we have the answers, and we've conveniently boiled them down to the Grand essentials below. You might want to print these out and leave them around the house, so the people you live with absorb them over time. A well-placed reminder of what makes you happy might spare them The Wrath. So everyone wins.

Checklist: What Irish Women Want

★ A nice cup of tea of course
★ A lie in on a Sunday
★ A grand foot rub after all the walking
★ Not to be invisible. Invisibility's a cool skill, but it gets old fast
★ Full reproductive rights, equal pay, y'know, full equality (Oh no you di'int! Oh yes we did.)
★ An annual government grant to go somewhere not damp
★ The right to be holy if we want to be, and the right to be profane if we're not
★ The perfect jumper. Not too hot, not too cold, not too scratchy, not too clingy, omnipresent: juuuust right
★ No more shushing
★ Loyalty. To us, of course, but also to brands. If you said you were a stout drinker, don't surprise us by telling us you've switched to a craft beer. We'll assume you're having an affair
★ The odd surprise trip to the west of Ireland
★ Sex. Duh
★ A call or text to let us know you're not dead. Preferably with a photo showing today's newspaper

★ Fairness
★ A hot drop from the pot

Now you know. Cut out and keep.

Grand Wisdom

•••••

Now we've shared our wisdom, you know you too are Grand. You are wise, like all Irish women. And it's your duty to bring other people to wisdom – even if they're not Irish, or women. Share the wealth, spread the love, be Grand. Tell them what you know. Tell them what you wish you'd known a lot earlier in your life. For instance:

★ Irish women wish we'd known … that if we didn't make the first move, Irish lads would never know we were interested.

★ We wish we'd known … that if we made the first move, some traditional Irish lads would lose interest. (Seriously, how did we ever get together at all?)

★ We wish we'd known … that to have an Irish number 1 single, you only have to sell about 11 copies. It would have maybe given us a bit more faith in our evolving tastes as the chart was topped yet again by Big Tom & The Mainliners.

★ We wish we'd known … that elderly relatives – while Peig-like – usually aren't around for too

much longer. Enjoy them while you can. Even if they play the accordion.

★ We wish we'd … learned how to drive as soon as possible. Rural public transport is terrible.

★ We wish we'd known … that we weren't really traitors if we chose not to eat meat sometimes. You can love Ireland and vegetables.

★ We wish we'd known … that masturbation didn't really make you go blind. Not til at least your mid-forties anyway.

★ We wish we'd known … how to knit. Making Aran jumpers would have made us all multi-billionaires by now and we wouldn't even have to worry about property bubbles.

★ We wish we'd known … that even if they're our elders, it's OK to tell sleazebags to piss off.

★ We wish we'd known … that the French are every bit as insecure as us underneath it all. We've collectively spent a lot of wasted time wishing we were from Paris.

★ We wish … we'd paid more attention in Irish class. It's a beautiful language and very handy when needing to talk about people on foreign holidays.

★ We wish we'd … written more stuff down. Only we really know what being an Irishwoman is all

about. Write stuff down. Scrawl it on a rock like our ancestors, if you have to. You'll forget. You will.

★ We wish we'd realised … that there were more flavours of ice-cream than "white", "pink", "pink & white", "kind of off-white" and "is that brown?"

★ We wish we'd … burnt every photo of ourselves as teenagers. They're still out there, somewhere. Probably in the iMOM database (a big box in the attic). And while we're on that topic …

★ We wish we'd … had more ritual burnings of photos. Or what younger modern Irish women call "deleting".

★ We wish we'd known straight off the bat that we were Grand, just the way we are. We are. You are. You're Grand.

Wrapping Up

• • • • •

Irish women have shuffled along for a long time with our heads down, against wind, rain and oppression. We've come an awful long way given that we can't always see where we're going with the mist. We hope we've shown you how we've not only survived but thrived under these conditions. Being Grand is almost never accidental. And now, you too have the keys. Use them wisely.

If there's an Irishwoman in your life, cherish her. She really

has to put up with an awful lot of shite. If you're an Irishwoman, you're never alone: your Grand sisters are with you. We've got your back. And if you're not an Irishwoman, you're still Grand. Everyone's welcome. Like we said, it's not like we don't have the space.

So let the women of the rest of the world get on with their searches for greatness: let the French be "merveilleuses", let Americans be "awesome". We're delighted for them. But we've got something which, while perhaps less impressive, will never fade with age and can never be taken away. It's part of who we are, and now we hope it's part of you. You're Grand.

We leave you with a proverb:

May the road rise before you, pothole and traffic free

May the wind be always at your back – it's kinder to the face, especially on a bike

May the sun shine warm upon your face and may the factor 50 never run low

And rains fall soft upon your fields so long as you've a grand pub nearby and the fire lit

And until we meet again (and we will, this place is ridiculously tiny)

May God hold you in the palm of Her hand.

Or whoever you're having yourself, we don't mind.

Either way, remember: You're Grand.

8

Grand Thanks

•••••

To the Irish and honorary Irish women in my life:
my iMOM, Mary and iFOD, Noel. My sister, Sara.
The aunties: Carmel, Trese, Ella, Anne M, Pat, Del,
Myriam and Anne D. The honorary aunties:
Clare, Heide and Monika. Real-life superheroines:
Brenda, Orlaith, Carrie, Maria, Wendy, Michelle,
Sharon, Shappi, Deirdre O'K, Tiffany and Kirsty.
To Diarmuid and Deirdre O'S. To John and Neil.
To John and Sebastian. To Bill and Kevin for
the quiet. To all at Mandy Ward Management
and Julian Benson Management. To Brendan, Ian,
Michelle and all at Dublin Comedy Improv.
To Ciara Considine and all at Hachette.
To Paul Howard for giving me the dare. And to the
American husband Carl for reminding me daily that no
matter what I might think, I'm actually Grand.

★